A Case Study of the Impact of Non-tariff Barriers on Trade Flow between Liberia and Nigeria (2015 - 2019)

A Case Study of the Impact of Non-tariff Barriers on Trade Flow between Liberia and Nigeria (2015 - 2019)

Ramses T. Kumbuyah

ISBN: 978-1-956736-34-2 (Paperback Edition)
ISBN: 978-1-956736-35-9 (Hardcover Edition)
ISBN: 978-1-956736-33-5 (E-book Edition)

Library of Congress Control Number: 2021920532

Book Ordering Information

Phone Number: 315 288-7939 ext. 1000 or 347-901-4920
Email: info@globalsummithouse.com
Global Summit House
www.globalsummithouse.com

Printed in the United States of America

CONTENTS

DECLARATIONS

Candidate's Declaration

I hereby declare that this Thesis was written by me and no part of this thesis was reproduced and / or presented to this University or any other institution of learning for another degree.

Candidate's Name: Ramses Tamba Kumbuyah

Candidate's Signature: _______________________ Date: 18/08/2021

Supervisor's Declaration

This is to certify that we have received and examined this thesis which was done by Ramses Tamba Kumbuyah under our supervision and have found that it is complete and satisfactory in all respects as required by the University of Liberia in partial fulfillment of the requirements for a Master of Arts Degree in International Relations and that any and all revisions required by the Thesis Review Committee have been made.

Supervisor's Name: Assistant Professor Thomas Kaydor, Jr.

Supervisor's Signature _______________________ Date: 18 Aug. 2021

Director of IBB's Name: Dr. Jonathan C. Taylor

Director of IBB's Signature: _______________________ Date: 18 Aug 2021

Vice President of Graduate Education's Name: Dr. Jonathan C. Taylor

Vice President of Graduate Education's Signature _______________ Date: 18 August 2021

i.

ABOUT THE AUTHOR

Ramses T. Kumbuyah is a Liberian. He was born unto the union of Mr. Saa Johnny Kumbuyah (deceased) and Madam Boika Sia Kumbuyah in Ndoliloe Village, Foya District, Lofa County, Republic of Liberia, West Africa on October 10, 1962. Ramses T. Kumbuyah started his early education at the Joseph Jenkins Roberts Elementary School, Kpormbu Town, Foya District in 1969 and completed six (6) grade in 1973. In 1974, he enrolled at the Tamba Taylor Public School in the seventh grade and completed junior high school in 1977 (with financial aid from the American Women in Liberia (very grateful). In 1978, he enrolled at the Voinjama

Multilateral High School in Lofa County where he stayed and completed 12th grade in 1980.

In 1982, Ramses T. Kumbuyah matriculated to the University of Liberia, pursuing his first college education. In 1986/87 he graduated with a B.Sc. Degree in Economics (minoring in Political Science). His quest for higher education had just begun. In 1996, he earned a Master in International Affairs (Economic Policy Management) Degree from the School of International and Public Affairs, Columbia University in the City of New York, USA (1994 – 1996) (thru a Joint Japan/ World Bank Scholarship (very grateful). In 2010, he earned an LLB Degree from the Louis Arthur Grimes School of Law, University of Liberia, and in 2021, earned a Master of Arts Degree in International Relations (with distinction) from the Ibrahim Badamasi Babangida (IBB) Graduate School of International Studies, University of Liberia. Ramses T. Kumbuyah also did short term courses at Oxford University - UK (Human Development Course) in 2004; ILO International Training Center, Turin Italy (Mitigating Job Crisis-Innovation in Public Employment Program Course) in 2010; World Bank Institute, Washington D.C. (Labor Market Policy Course) in 2012; and Georgetown University in Washington D.C, USA (Coalition Building Course) in 2014.

Ramses T. Kumbuyah started professional work in Liberia with the Ministry of Planning and Economic Affairs in 1987 as a Research Officer in the External Aid Section of the Ministry. He was promoted to Senior Research Officer, then Assistant Minister/ Special Assistant to the Minister (1997 – 1999). At the Ministry of Finance, he served as Coordinator for International Economic Cooperation (1999 - 2000); the Liberia Agency of Community Empowerment (LACE) as Executive Director (2005 – 2013); the Ministry of Education as Deputy Minister for Administration (2013 – 2015); National Bureau of Concessions as Deputy Director General for Concessions (2015 – 2019); and the Law Reform Commission as Executive Director, a.i. (2020 – Present).

In the private sector, Ramses T. Kumbuyah worked with the Century Law Office, and then with the Galaxy & Associates Inc. as Associate Lawyer in Monrovia, Liberia. With international organizations, he worked with UNDP-Liberia as National Economist (2000 – 2005); (USAID/ Development Alternative Initiative (DAI) /Liberia Accountability and Voice Initiative (LAVI) /the Liberian Legislature's House Standing Committee on Elections and Inauguration (HSCEI) Election Support Project as Independent Consultant for legislative drafting (2019-2020); and the World Bank, Washington D.C as Intern (1996), and World Bank's Health and Nutrition Project in Tanzania (1996)) as Consultant/health sector planning; and at the University of Liberia, Economics Department as Instructor II, teaching Principles of Economics, Statistics and Microeconomics (1997 – 1998). Ramses T. Kumbuyah has worked as an administrator, economist, teacher, community empowerment (social infrastructure) practitioner, and youth employment (public works) practitioner. He is strong in concept development and literary works.

DEDICATION

I dedicate this thesis to my wife, Christine S. Kumbuyah, for allowing me undertake this study, for her motivation and support; to my children (Lucretia (deceased), Comfort, Magdalene, Ketura, Marian; Rebecca, Seitta and Kumbuyah Jr.) for encouraging me up to the end, and to my mother, Sia Boika, and my sister, Ma-Mary Kumba for their best wishes and prayers for me during the course of my sojourn. I am so grateful to all of you.

ACKNOWLEDGEMENT

I wish to thank my Professors that taught me during my study at the IBB Graduate School. These professors include, but not limited to, Assistant Professor. Thomas Kaydor, Amb. Nathaniel M. Barnes, Prof. Josephus M. Gray, Dr. Tanya Ansahta Garnett, and Dr. Johnathan C. Taylor. I wish to appreciate them for impacting knowledge into me during my pursuit of studies for a Master of Arts Degree in International Relations at the Ibrahim Badamasi Babangida Graduate School of International Studies at the University of Liberia. Indeed, teaching is a selfless service, and their sacrifices in impacting knowledge have to be acknowledged.

Again, I am especially grateful to my Assistant Professor and Thesis Supervisor, Assistant Professor Thomas Kaydor for his professional advice while writing this thesis. I am also grateful to him for accepting at short notice to advise me. His guidance and commitment indeed help me to complete this task successfully.

Finally, I want to acknowledge my Lord Jesus Christ, who knows all things and provides for his own in keeping with his riches in glory. I am thankful to the Almighty God for the gift of knowledge, wisdom and understanding.

ABSTRACT

This qualitative study assessed the impact of Non-tariff Barriers (NTBs) on trade flow within ECOWAS, focusing especially on trade flow between Liberia and Nigeria. The exploratory research designed was used for this study. The target population was the members of the Liberian Marketing Association (LMA) (Waterside Branch) that has a total membership of 45,000 market men, women and youth. The research sample size of thirty (30) respondents was drawn from the membership of the LMA (Waterside branch). Of the thirty respondents, 15 provided answers to the open-ended questions, while the other 15 respondents participated in the focus group discussion.

The Study shows that indeed there exists NTBs that inhibit the free flow of trade within the sub-region, and between Liberia and Nigeria. The main NTBs identified are (1) long custom procedures at the posts of entry between the six West African Countries; the customs officers and security officers demand extra payments for goods in transit; (2) the high-level of corruption and bribery on the highway and check points, demanding money from the traders; and (3) extorting money for stamping the ECOWAS Passport, which should not be the case. The study concluded that until the NTBs are removed or mitigated, trade flow between Liberia and Nigeria, and within ECOWAS will remain marginal. The study therefore recommended some non-tariff measures (operational) and policy reforms in order to remove the NTBs or mitigate their effect on trade flow. The three major recommendations are: (a) requesting payments for stamping of the ECOWAS Passport should be stopped because the money does not go into the coffers of the governments; (b) that the governments of Liberia, Cote d'Ivoire, Ghana, Togo and Nigeria should improve services at their respective customs border posts; (c) The governments of the two countries (Liberia and Nigeria) should review their local trade policies and take steps to increasing trade between the two countries.

CHAPTER ONE: INTRODUCTION

1.0 Introduction

This Chapter is the introductory part of this thesis. The thesis examines the impact of Non-tariff Barriers on the flow of trade within the ECOWAS sub-region, with Liberia and Nigeria as a case study for the period 2015 – 2019. The Chapter discusses the background, the problem statement, the purpose and objectives of the study, the significance of the study, the research question as well as the scope of the study. The Chapter concludes with the definition of terms, and a section on the organization of the study.

1.1 Background of the Study

Trade has been an indispensable part of human existence, from the barter system to the modern system of exchange. The evolution of trade can be seen through various trade theories from ancient to modern times. The Scottish and English Political Economist in the 18th and 19th centuries, Barnand Mandeville (1714/ 1970) in the "Fable of the Bees" argued that "the actions of self-interest free individuals and is also good for society". The Scottish moral philosopher articulated a theory of subjectivity, theorizing desire self-interest and virtue. (Knowing the Third World: Colonial Encounter (Anonymous, p. 55).

For his part, Adam Smith (1776, Wealth of Nations Book 1, Chapter 2) developed the economic theory of the "invisible hand". He articulated that "it is not from the benevolence of the brewer or the baker that we expect our dinner, but from their regard for their own self-interest". Adam Smith's concept of "invisible hand" was the foundation for capitalism; that self-interest is the motive for private investment for wealth maximization, which benefits society at large (Knowing The Third World, Colonial Encounter, p.55).

The concept of deployment of labour beyond borders in order to increase the production of goods and services was propagated by David Ricardo (1817-1951). He stressed "how societies' production of industrial goods could be multiplied not in one country alone but in many, almost without any assignable limit if disposed to bestow the labour necessary to obtain them" (Knowing The Third World, Colonial Encounter, p. 60). Mr. David Ricardo also popularized a "model of Free Trade within the concept of comparative advantage" (Krugman and Obstfeld, 1994, pp. 11 - 12). The theory states that if two countries, for example, were together producing two goods, then a greater total quantity of both goods could be produced if each country completely specializes in producing the goods that could be produced with relatively less labour domestically than any other strategy.

Within the context of global trade, numerous studies have shown that the developing countries are at disadvantage when negotiating with the developed countries. The developing countries have no control over prices for imports and exports on the world market (Irogbe, 2005 pp. 42-44). The developing countries hardly achieve their desire trade objectives in terms of tariff negotiations. The making of basic decisions in the world market is determined by the dominant nations. The General Agreement on Tariffs and Trade (GATT) was established in October 1947, which was later transformed into the World Trade Organization (WTO) (Shukla, 2000, p. 1), with the objective to reduce tariffs and allow free flow of goods and services between and among nations. The GATT was formed following decades of unsatisfactory trade and monetary relations, marked by "Beggar-thy-Neighbor" policies (Shukla, 2000, p.1). However, the unfavorable manipulation of the international export and import markets by the superpower countries continued under the World Trading Organization (WTO). Under the WTO rules, the interest of the superpowers was almost always protected. For instance, where developed countries had to meet the import and/or export requirements, the different rules and exemptions under the GATT/WTO rules would be used to meet the interest of the major super powers. For example, the Most Favored Nation (MFN) status could be invoked in order to accommodate the trading objectives of a superpower. Also, a Non-tariff Barrier (NTB) such as the Sanitary and Phytosanitary Standards, especially for animal products would be imposed against developing countries in order to stop or limit their exports from entering the markets of the developed countries.

The world market has almost always operated at the expense of the developing countries. Between 1984 and 1994, GATT became unable to effectively function. In addition to unequal treatment of developing countries vis-à-vis developed countries, there were issues in agriculture (e.g. quantitative measures); and discriminatory and restrictive issues on textiles and clothing, that GATT could not resolve because it was against the interest of the European Countries (Shukla, 2000, pp.9-10). As a result, developing countries began to request for reform of the world trading system, especially following the release of the Haberler Report, which revealed that "the problem of the underdeveloped world was due, in a no small measure, to the trade policies of the developed countries" (Shukla 2000, p.7). In April 1994, in Marrakesh (Morocco), the World Trade Organization (WTO) was established to replace the GATT (Shukla, 2000, p. 26).

Unlike the GATT, the WTO system did not limit itself to cross-border transactions in tangible goods but also in intangibles such as services. The WTO brought in reforms in agriculture, textiles and clothing as well as trade system issues.

In light of the unfavorable trade arrangements against the developing countries under the GATT, and failure of GATT to effectively deal with the concerns of the developing countries, regional trading blocs began to be formed by developing countries in order to benefit from intra-regional trade. In Africa, for example, the East African Community (EAC), the Southern African Development Community (SADC), and the Economic Community of West African States (ECOWAS) were formed with the objectives of eliminating tariffs amongst member states in the regional groupings, maintaining a Common External Tariff (CET) against non-members, and creating a free trade area (Keane, Cali & Kenneh, 2010, pp. 2, 27) (Mwasha, 2007, p. 2). There were also attempts by the leaders of Africa to create Africa's Continental Free Trade Area, (Rodrik, Abstract, 1998, p.5), thus bringing all states of Africa into one market.

ECOWAS was established in 1975 with the goal to creating a customs union; to eliminate all tariffs, and ensure the free flow of goods and services within its member states. Working towards this direction, ECOWAS adopted two trade policies known as the ECOWAS Trade Liberalization Scheme (ETLS) and the Common External Tariff (CET). However, trade experts criticized the non-performance of these trade policies due to the lack of commitment by member countries (https://www.ecowas.int/ecowas-sectors/trade/) to implement them.

Nonetheless, another factor affecting the flow of trade within the West African sub-region has been the existence of Non-tariff Barriers (NTBs). Some of the NTBs include the high level of highway bribery and corruption, non-compliance with the rule of origin of goods, the lack of modern infrastructure like seaports to facilitate trade within the region, quotas and subsidies for exports and imports, as well as domestic national economic and trade policies. These NTBs contribute to the low level of trade between and among ECOWAS member states. For example, trade level between Liberia and Nigeria is very marginal. Nigeria is the largest market within the ECOWAS sub-region with over a hundred million consumers, but Liberia's share of trade in ECOWAS was reported as 1.1% imports and 0.2% exports between 2005 to 2009. As for Nigeria, the trade percentage share of imports was 12.5%. and 44.7% exports during the same periods. Nigeria exports more in the sub-region than imports (Keane, Cali and Kennan, 2010 pp 11-13).

The low intra-ECOWAS trade could partly be due to poor infrastructure and the lack of uniform standards relative to the importation of animal and poultry products, i.e., the Sanitary and Phytosanitary Standards(SPS). Also, there is a high level of informal trading in the sub-region, couple with the high level of corruption and bribery on the highways, which undermine the magnitude of trade flow amongst and between countries of ECOWAS, and clog the movement of people and goods across borders.

With the numerous NTBs, Liberia has been unable to effectively take advantage of the vast Nigerian market. Liberia launched a new trade policy, the Liberian National Trade Policy (LNTP, 2014 - 2019), and has been making effort to meeting the WTO post-accession requirements (Liberia National Trade Policy, 2014) (Annual Reports, Ministry of Commerce and Industry 2016, 2017). Liberia has also demonstrated its commitment to adhering to the ECOWAS Trade Liberalization Scheme (ETLS) and the Common External Tariff (CET). However, technical barriers, such as the non-certification of the Liberian National Standard Laboratory (NSL) make it difficult for the country to access international markets under the WTO mechanism. Other restraining NTBs are the ineffective implementation of the rules of origin, and Liberia's inability to meet the ECOWAS Agriculture Policy and the WTO Requirements for the exportation of plants and animal products. The NSL has not met international standards, and hence cannot certificate products from Liberia for export.

1.2 Statement of the Problem

The goal of regional trade organizations, such as ECOWAS is to eliminate tariff and to ensure a free flow of exports and imports within member states. Nonetheless, most regional organizations in Africa, especially ECOWAS have not been able to achieve this goal. The ECOWAS member states, have not been able to effectively implement the ECOWAS Trade Liberation Scheme (ETLS) and/or the ECOWAS Common External Tariff (CET). As such, the trade flow amongst and between member states (e.g., Liberia and Nigeria) remain low (Keane, Cali & Kennan 2010, pp. 8-9). Many ECOWAS' reports show that Nigeria's intra-ECOWAS trade is marginal compared to trade with Europe, Asia and the Americas. This was attributed, inter alia, to the prevalence of the NTBs in the sub-region (Harris, Chmbers and Foresti, 2011) (https://www.ecowas.int/ecowas-sectors/trade/) (see Appendix D). The Non-tariff Barriers (NTBs) have become binding constraints on trade, and limit the gains from trade. There is a wide range of NTBs, some of which unnecessarily restrict trade flow and undermine gains from trade liberalization and diversification of products and markets. Therefore, this study examines the impact of NTBs on trade flow within ECOWAS, especially between Liberia and Nigeria; the impact of NTBs on the growth of trade and commerce within in the sub-region, and on the traders, in terms of business constraints and /or opportunity lost.

1.3 Purpose and Objectives of the Study

Currently, there are just too many NTBs that are hindering trade flow within the ECOWAS sub-regions (Harris, Chambers and Foresti, 2011). NTBs have been defined as unnecessarily restrictive non-tariff measures (NTMs) which affect trade flow in goods and services. The presence of NTBs can undermine gains from trade liberalization for new entrants, and also constrain trade diversification efforts across products and markets (Keane, Cali & Kennan, 2010, p. vi). Some of the NTBs are government policies, technical regulations, quantitative restrictions such as quotas, licensing processes, long custom procedures, border tax adjustments, limited private sector knowledge about ECOWAS trade protocols, bribery and corruption at checkpoints, lack of certification under the Sanitary and Phyto-sanitary Standards (SPS) requirements, poor infrastructure, among others. Therefore, the purpose of this study is:

(1) To assess the impact of the Non-tariff Barriers (NTBs) on trade flow within the ECOWAS sub-region, especially between Liberia and Nigeria;

(2) To assess the impact of the NTBs on the traders/marketers who traveled between Liberia and Nigeria;

(3) To identify the NTBs that need to be reformed or eliminated in order for trade to flow between Liberia and Nigeria; and,

(4) To identify the policies of Liberia and Nigeria that should be reformed in order for trade to flow freely between the two countries.

The overall objective of this study is to provide evidence-based solution to solving the NTBs problem in the ECOWAS sub-region, especially in Liberia and Nigeria. The study will engender a debate on reform measures relative to creating an enabling environment for free trade in the ECOWAS sub-region by reforming trade policies and protocols, and removing artificial NTBs.

1.4 Research Questions

The key Research Question for this study is "how are NTBs negatively impacting the flow of trade between Liberia and Nigeria"? The four (4) sub-questions connected to the objective are as follows:

(1) What are the NTBs that are negatively impacting trade flow between Liberia and Nigeria?

(2) How are the NTBs affecting the traders/marketers who traveled between Liberia and Nigeria?

(3) What are the NTBs that need to be reformed in order for trade to flow freely between Liberia and Nigeria, and within ECOWAS? and,

(4) What national policy reform measures that should be undertaken in order to improve trade flow between Liberia and Nigeria, and within ECOWAS as a whole?

1.5 Significance of the Study

Trade flow between Nigeria and Liberia has a potential to grow and create wealth for the business people of the two countries, enhance economies of scale, provide affordable goods for consumers and tariff revenue for the governments of both countries. However, Non-tariff Barriers are unintended and unnecessary restrictions on trade flow. For the most part, Non-tariff Barriers stifle the growth of trade. Therefore, this study is significant because:

(1) It will enable policy makers, especially in Liberia, Nigeria and ECOWAS, to re-look at their trade policies in order to ascertain as to whether they are indeed facilitating trade, meeting the objectives of ECOWAS and the WTO, or need to be reformed.

(2) Local business associations wanting to reform the NTBs, i.e., government's trade policies, ECOWAS protocols, and/or WTO rules can use this evidence-based study to champion their cause for reform;

(3) The business people wanting to protect local industries and expand their access to global markets can use this study to lobby their Lawmakers to enact or amend relevant trade/ investment codes, and

(4) This study leaves room for further research on other aspects of trade, thus widening the scope of knowledge on the subject of trade; for example, why the ECOWAS member countries have not acceded fully to the ECOWAS Common External Tariff?

1.6 The Limitation of the Study

Because of financial resource constraint, this research was done solely in Liberia. The researcher did not travel to Nigeria to collect samples. All data collection was done in Liberia. Respondents were drawn from the business community, mainly ordinary marketers who traveled between Liberia and Nigeria for business purposes. The target respondents were business people but yet they allotted time to answer to the interview questions; while others participated in the focus group discussions. The researcher experienced resistance and non-compliance from some of the target respondents, not wanting to leave their businesses to participate in the focus group discussions. The researcher was faced with financial constraint to cover the cost of printing and binding of this thesis.

1.7 Delimitation of the Study

For this study on the impact of NTBs on trade flow between Liberia and Nigeria, the research was limited to analyzing the effect of NTBs that affect trade flow within ECOWAS, but mainly between the two countries, assessing the impact of NTBs on the trade route from Liberia (Monrovia) to Loguato Border, to Danane (Cote d'Ivoire border with Liberia), then through the highway to Abidjan; then from Abidjan to Noway (Cote D'Ivoire – Ghana border). From there through Accra to Ghana - Togo border; then to Togo – Benin border, and then to Benin - Nigerian border, and finally into Nigeria for business. This route is followed when returning from Nigeria to Monrovia (Liberia). This route is the main trading route between the two countries. The respondents were drawn from the local business community; the business people that traveled between Liberia and Nigeria, as well as other parts of the ECOWAS sub-region for business purposes. From the target population of the Liberian Marketing Association (LMA) (Waterside Branch), which was estimated at 45,000 marketers, a sample size of thirty (30) respondents was drawn. A simple random sampling technique was used to collect the sample size. Two instruments were used for data collection: self-developed open-ended questions, and focus group discussion. The objective was to increase the veracity of the responses to the open-ended questions.

In terms of content, although the ECOWAS trade protocols were reviewed, the focus of the study remained the Non-tariff Barriers (NTBs).

The research reflected on why nations trade, the gains from trade; the ECOWAS trade objectives, and then the NTBs that limit the flow of trade between Liberia and Nigeria. The study also reviewed the ECOWAS Trade Liberalization Scheme and the challenges of implementation. Although the study was based on international trade theory and policies, the objective was not to delve into complex econometric modeling nor test of hypothesis. The objective was to identify gabs in the implementation of ETLS, ECOWAS trade protocols, and the effect and treatment of the NTBs.

1.8 Definitions of Key Terms

Common External Tariff (CET) is an import tariff applied equally by member states of a customs union (e.g. ECOWAS) on goods imported, regardless of which country the imports are entering the union.

Customs Union is generally a type of trade bloc which is composed of a free trade area with a CET. A customs union is established through trade agreements, where the participating countries set up CET and other trade policies.

ECOWAS Trade Liberalization Scheme (ETLS) is an agreement amongst member states to liberalize trade within the West African sub-region, in terms of establishing a common market through the abolition amongst member states of custom duties, levies on imports and exports, as well as the abolition of Non-tariff Barriers.

Free Trade Area is a region encompassing a trade bloc, whose member states signed a free trade agreement (FTA) to reduce trade barriers, import quotas and tariffs, and to increase trade in goods and services amongst themselves.

The General Agreement on Tariffs and Trade (GATT) is a legal agreement amongst states whose overall purpose is to promote international trade by reducing or eliminating trade barriers such as tariffs and quotas.

Most Favored Nation (MFN) is a trading mechanism under the WTO agreement that requires every member state to treat other countries equally. Countries are not allowed to discriminate between their trading partners; granting a special favour such as reducing customs duty rate for one of their partners would require that it be done for all other WTO members.

National Treatment under the WTO principles means that all traders should be treated equally; it does not matter whether they are local or foreign companies. Trade incentives provided to local firms must also be provided to foreign firms.

Non-tariff Barriers (NTBs) are barriers that restricts imports or exports of goods or services through mechanism other than the simple imposition of tariff.

Rules of Origin is a criteria set by a customs union to determine the national source of a product. This is important because customs duty charges depend on the source of the import, whether or not the goods are locally produced. Goods locally produced in a member state of the customs union are exempt from custom duties or levies, and are allowed to be traded freely within the customs union.

Reciprocity is one of the fundamental principles under the GATT/WTO, which refers to the idea of mutual exchange in trade policy, that would bring about changes in the volume of each country imports that are of equal value to the changes in the volume of its exports, thus the concessions are balanced or reciprocal.

Sanitary and Phyto-sanitary Standards (SPS) are measures under the WTO requirements that are put in place to protect human, animals, and plants from diseases, pests, or contaminants.

Trade Barriers are governments' imposed restrictions on international trade. Tariffs are barriers that increase the cost of imports; and Non-tariff Barriers are non-tariffs measures that restrict imports and sometimes exports, e.g., export ban, long customs procedures, imports and export quotas.

World Trade Organization (WTO) is an inter-governmental organization that deals with the global rule of trade between countries. Its main function is to ensure that trade flow as smoothly, predictably and freely as possible.

1.9 Organization of the study

This study is divided into five (5) chapters. Chapter One looks at the background of the study, the statement of the problem, the purpose and objectives of the study, research questions, the significance of the study, the scope (limitation and delimitation) of the study, definition of key words, and lastly the organization of the study.

Chapter Two covers Literature Review, which provides the conceptual review and explanation of the study. The Chapter provides information on prior studies on the subject matter. It reviews existing literary and research studies of other scholars on the topic studied, i.e., the Impact of Non-tariff Barriers on trade flow within the ECOWAS Sub-region, a case study of trade flow between Liberia and Nigeria.

Chapter Three presents the methodology of the study, which includes the target population of the study, the research method, the research design, sample size, sampling technique, instruments and data collection and analysis procedures.

Chapter Four covers data presentation, interpretation and data analysis. While Chapter Five provides key findings, conclusion and recommendation of the study.

CHAPTER TWO: REVIEW OF RELATED LITERATURE

2.0 Introduction

This Chapter discusses a review of related literature. The literature review helps to identify data sources that other researchers have used; it enables the researcher to review prior works and identify gabs in the literature. In this Chapter, the literature relating to trade policies of Liberia and Nigeria (our case study), the Non-tariff Barriers (NTBs) as well as the policies of trade facilitating institutions, such as ECOWAS, WTO and related sub-regional organizations, were reviewed. This section identified relevant theoretical and conceptual frameworks, defining the research question, which lay the foundation for the study, inspired new areas for the research, and identified gabs and inconsistencies in the body of research.

2.1 Evolution of Trade Theories

The evolution of trade has its genesis in ancient times. The development of trade is seen through the lenses of the evolution of trade theories. Development during the ancient times was typically associated with the violence of colonization, gunboat diplomacy, and wars between superpowers (Anonymous, Knowing the Third World: Colonial Encounters, p. 54). The struggle for domestic development by the superpowers (Britain, the Americas, and

Europe) led to impoverishment and external control over domestic affairs, the dissolution of indigenous institutions and culture, and environmental deterioration in developing countries.

The concept of land as a factor of production was introduced by Mr. John Locke, an ancient Economist. Mr. Locke argued that "man's labor exerted over an inert nature creates value that gives individuals the right to possess the nature they had thereby improved". Mr. Locke further argued that "private property was necessary to realize individual freedom" (Aonymous, Knowing the Third World: Colonial Encounters, p. 54). Mr. Locke's point was buttressed by the "Physiocrats." The Physiocrats argued that "the sole source of economic growth for a nation lay in exploiting the land – a natural resource provided freely by nature".

On his part, the Scottish and English Political Economist in the 18th and 19th Centuries, Mr. Barnand Mandeville (1714-1970), in the "Fable of the Bees", argued that "the action of self- interest free individuals and is also good for society". The Scottish moral philosopher, Mr. Mandeville, articulated a theory of subjectivity, theorizing desire self-interest and virtue (Anonymous, Knowing the Third World: Colonial Encounters, p. 55). The origin of the concept of capitalism is credited to the British Political Economist, Adam Smith (1776) through his theory of the "invisible hand" in his book the Wealth of Nations (Book 1, Chapter 2). He articulated that "it is not from the benevolence of the brewer, or the baker that we expect our dinner, but from their regard for their own self-interest (Aonymous, Knowing the Third World: Colonial Encounters, p. 55). Adam Smith's concept of invisible hand was the foundation for capitalism. He noted that self-interest is the motive for private investment and wealth maximization, which benefit the society at large.

Mr. Adam Smith made further contribution to the trade theory. He introduced the second factor of production. He recognized that human labor is a necessary input to producing an economic surplus (Anonymous, Knowing the Third World: Colonial Encounters, p. 60). Mr. Smith saw the difference between developed and less developed world as lying in the skill dexterity and judgment with which labor was applied.

Mr. David Ricardo (1871- 1951) projected the concept of deployment of labour beyond borders in order to increase the production of goods and services (Anonymous, Knowing the Third World: Colonial Encounters, p. 60). He stressed "how societies production of industrial goods could be multiplied not in one country alone, but in many, almost without any assignable limit if disposed to bestow the labour necessary to obtain them." Mr. David Ricardo also popularized the Model of Free Trade within the concept of comparative advantage (Krugman and Obsfield, 1994, pp. 11-12). The theory states that if two countries, for example, were together producing two goods, then a greater total quantity of both goods could be produced if each country completely specializes in producing the goods that could be produced with relatively less labour domestically than any other strategy".

On the other hand, the Economic Historians, Mr. Watt Rostow, ushered in the modern theories of economic development and trade. Mr. Rostow envisioned five stages through which a society passes from traditional characteristics to maturity (Aonymous, Knowing the Third World: Development Decades, pp. 70-71). The characteristics are: (1) traditional society; (2) pre-condition for take-up; (3) the take-off stage, (4) the drive to maturity, (5) the age of high mass consumption, (6) and beyond mass consumption. Essentially, Mr. Rostow was "asserting that consumer demand, entrepreneurship and technical knowledge can push the economy towards optimum path of growth of each sector", and he further implied that national economic growth is governed by a dynamic tendency towards the optimum path, though can be interrupted by external shocks.

A Chinese Economist, Mr. Cao Fangiun, for his part defined modern society as a society where manufacturing and service sectors have absolute advantage over the other sectors (Fangium, 2009, p. 8). The ratio of reliance upon inanimate energy is much higher relative to animate energy in the modern society. One of the notable futures of a modernized society is rapid advancement of science and technology, which rapidly increase industrialization and automation. Mr. Fangiun further argued that modern societies are highly stratified in social structure, i.e., various organizations are specialized and interdependent. Individual roles and social status are highly defined by their abilities and achievements (Fangium, 2009, p. 8). The concepts of modern culture include rationalism, individual freedom, competitive spirit, and emphases on efficiency and functionality.

2.2 The Growth of International Trade and the Need for Control

Some of the questions that developing countries continue to ask are that: First, "to what extent do the developing countries benefit from the growth of international trade since the end of World War II"? The World War II saw the formation of the Bretton Woods Institutions, the IMF and the World Bank, as a framework for the rebuilding of Europe. Second, how is globalization helping the developing countries? Third, how are trade policies of GATT and the WTO helping developing countries gain from international trade policies, given their weak negotiating position?

In an attempt to provide some answers to the questions above, Mr. Kima Irogbe (Professor of Political Science at Claflin University (USA, 2005) argued that the socio-economic and political structure of peripheral countries are subordinated through globalization to foster the economic interest of the metropolitan countries (Irogbe, 2005 p.41). Mr. Theotonio Dos Santos, a Brazilian Social Scientist, affirmed that "because of the unequal political, military and economic relationship between a dependent economy and a dominant external economy, the structure of the dependent economy is shaped as much or more by the requirement of the external economy. Further, due to globalization, the economy of the dependent would be impossible to maintain without the existence and support of the external factors (Irogbe, 2005, pp. 42-43). As such, the entrepreneurs of the underdeveloped countries have no control over international markets for their primary products and prices; and often result to unfavorable terms of trade for imports in underdeveloped countries.

Some economists attribute the lack of competitiveness of developing countries to dependency. The development alternatives open to dependent countries are defined and limited by integration into, and functions within the world market. The limitations of alternatives for developing countries differ from the limitation in the developed countries, in as much as the functioning decision of the world market are determined by the developed countries.

Therefore, the dependent countries must make choices in the situation where they do not set the terms or parameters of choice (Irogbe, 2005, p. 44). Now, let's look at trade facilitating institutions put in place by the Americans and Europeans after the Second World War.

2.2.1. General Agreement on Tariffs and Trade (GATT) /World Trade Organization (WTO)

At the end of World War II, twenty-three countries, led primarily by the United States, Canada, and the United Kingdom, negotiated the General Agreement on Tariffs and Trade (GATT) on October 30, 1947. The goal was to reach an agreement that would ensure postwar stability, and avoid a repeat of the mistakes of the past, including the Smoot-Hawley tariffs and retaliatory responses (The WTO and GATT: A Principled History, p. 11), which was a contributing factor to the devastating economic climate following the Second World War. In 1947, GATT created a new basic template of rules and exceptions to regulate international trade between members (referred to as contracting parties) and stipulated the initial tariffs. The main objective of GATT was tariffs reduction (Shukla 2000, p. 5). The eight basic principles of GATT were (1) non-discrimination, (2) prohibition of quantitative restrictions and acceptance of tariffs, (3) the principle of national treatment, (4) reciprocity in tariff negotiations, (5) retaliation, (6) safeguard mechanism, (7) international cross border trade, and (8) voting rights, decision making procedures, and amendment procedures (Shukla 2000, pp. 2-3).

The twenty-three countries that participated in the Geneva negotiations (The WTO and GATT: A Principled History, p. 11) that led to the signing of the GATT in 1947 were Australia, Belgium, Brazil, Burma (Myanmar), Canada, Ceylon (Sri Lanka), Chile, China, Cuba, Czechoslovakia (Czech Republic and Slovakia), France, India, Lebanon, Luxembourg, Netherlands, New Zealand, Norway, Pakistan, South Africa, Southern Rhodesia (Zimbabwe), Syria, United Kingdom, and United States.

Over the next forty-seven years, more countries signed on to the GATT, and more trade liberalization negotiations were pursued. Between 1947 and 1994, the GATT Contracting Parties began and concluded eight separate negotiating rounds of voluntary trade liberalization. The last of these completed rounds was the Uruguay Round (The WTO and GATT: A Principled History, p. 12), which ended the GATT era in 1994 by ushering in the World Trade Organization (WTO). By 1994, the GATT membership had simultaneously expanded from the initial 23 Contracting Parties to 128 participating countries. With a number of new members acceding to the WTO since its 1994 inception, more than 150 countries have signed the agreement in order to promote global trade facilitation and policies.

2.2.2. The Negotiating Rounds and Negotiating Approaches

The GATT rules for trade were only good enough for developed countries. The first five rounds of GATT negotiations, covering the initial 1947 to 1961 period, were typically dominated by major exporting countries, and those with a "principal supplying interest" in a particular product (The WTO and GATT: A Principled History, p. 12), getting together and negotiating reciprocal market access improvements. In order to further legitimize their grip on global trade policies, the European and American Economists and trade experts provided justification for certain policies of GATT that favor suppliers of the developed countries. (The WTO and GATT: A Principled History, p. 12)

For instance, the European and American Trade experts discussed not only the negotiating history but also the economic outcomes of different negotiating approaches of principal suppliers versus tariff formulas and exemptions. They provided an economic theory that rationalizes participation by the largest exporters in the negotiations (The WTO and GATT: A Principled History, p. 12) and thus supported the principal supplier rule as a feature of the negotiations. These theories justified the "principal supplier rule" as a means to overcome their concerns about externalities that could lead to the failure of multilateral negotiations caused by the "free rider problem". Accordingly, in GATT, those with principal supplying interest were the developed economies, mainly the Americans and the Europeans. They focused their negotiation efforts on reducing import barriers in other countries that were of primary interest to their own exporters (The WTO and GATT: A Principled History, p. 13). The developed countries used their political trade-off to expand market access abroad for exporting industries against increased market access granted at home to foreign industries. Thus, industries of developing countries competing against imports of developed countries experienced losses. In other words, since most developing countries were neither principal suppliers nor major importing markets, little was asked of them in terms of their own trade liberalization; and little of what was of direct export interest to developing countries was liberalized by others.

2.2.3. Important Commercial Sector Exemptions to the GATT

In addition to the general problem of certain products effectively being excluded from multilateral trade liberalization rounds, because of the principal supplier interest and formula-exemption approaches to the GATT negotiations, the contracting parties deepened the severity of the problem (The WTO and GATT: A Principled History, p. 14) in certain sectors by essentially taking two industries off the negotiating table: agriculture, apparel and textiles. First, beginning with the 1950s, many agricultural trades were exempt from GATT discipline. The United States initiated the trend by requesting a GATT waiver to that effect; the emerging European Economic Community subsequently supported this decision as it undertook substantial government interventions in agricultural markets (The WTO and GATT: A Principled History, p. 14) through its Common Agricultural Policy (CAP). This lack of discipline concerning trade in agricultural products ultimately resulted in the overlapping of domestic policies throughout the sector, thus increasing import restrictions as well as substantial domestic support (subsidies) programs. The lack of discipline also led to choking effect on import, and made suppliers artificially competitive in third country (export) markets (The WTO and GATT: A Principled History, p. 14).

Second, with the accession of Japan to the GATT in 1955, special trading rules were introduced to deal with potentially disruptive imports in clothing and textile products. What began as a short-term arrangement, covering cotton and textiles in 1961, was turned into a long-term arrangement (1962–73) (The WTO and GATT: A Principled History, p. 15) and subsequently the Multifibre Arrangement (MFA) (1974–94). These agreements managed global textiles and apparel trade through a complex system of quantitative restrictions and voluntary export restraints. The products covered by these agreements thus fell outside of the GATT system of rules, discipline and ultimately enforcement (The WTO and GATT: A Principled History, P. 15).

2.2.4. The GATT and WTO fundamental principles

The original GATT principles, on which the GATT and the WTO were built are reciprocity, most-favored-nation treatment, and national treatment (Shukla, 2000, pp.2-3) (The WTO and

GATT: A Principled History, pp. 15-17). These principles are of practical relevance for shaping the outcomes of negotiations, their impact on government policies, and subsequently on trade flow and economic activity. In most instances, the WTO principles were used by the developed countries to seek further market access in the developing counties. On the contrary, developing countries were unable to effectively negotiate or bargain because they were neither principal suppliers nor major importers, and therefore their import and export market concerns could be ignored.

2.3 The Development of Regional Trading Blocs and their Policies

2.3.1 Africa Continental Free Trade Agreement (AfCFTA)

The 18th Ordinary Session of the Assembly of Heads of State and Governments of the African Union, held in Addis Ababa, Ethiopia in January 2012, adopted a decision to establish a Continental Free Trade Area (AfCFTA). The Summit also endorsed the Action Plan on Boosting Intra-Africa Trade (BIAT) which identifies seven priority action clusters: trade policy, trade facilitation, productive capacity, trade related infrastructure, trade finance, trade information, and factor market integration. (African Continental Free Trade Area (AfCFTA) Legal Texts and Policy Documents) (https://www.tralac.org/resources/by-region/ cfta. html#ratification). African leaders launched the operational phase of the new African Continental Free Trade Area (AfCFTA) at the 12th Extraordinary African Union Summit on 7 July 2019 in Niamey, Niger. The AfCFTA is being governed by five operational instruments, i.e., the Rules of Origin, the online negotiating forum, the monitoring and elimination of Non-tariff Barriers, a digital payments system, and the African Trade Observatory (https:// www.tralac.org/resources/by-region/cfta.html#ratification). The 54-nation trade bloc is set to become the biggest integrated market worldwide, uniting some 2.5 billion people by 2050 (http://www..west-africa-brief.org/content/en/west-africa-african-continental-free-trade-area International Journal of Economics and Finance; Vol. 4, No. 10; 2012). Under the AfCFTA, member states committed themselves to eliminate tariffs on most goods, which is expected to increase trade in the region sustainably in the medium term. The African Union's goal was to make the free-trade area instruments operational by July 2020, but this has not been achieved.

Ghana was chosen to host AfCFTA's permanent secretariat, placing the country at the heart of the continental integration process. Nigeria – along with Benin – signed the AfCFTA agreement a few hours ahead of the AU Summit in Niamey. The Agreement establishing the African Continental Free Trade Area (AfCFTA) entered into force on 30th May 2019, when 24 countries deposited their instruments of ratification. This date marked 30 days after 22 countries had deposited their ratification instruments with the African Union Commission (AUC) chairperson, the designated depository for this purpose, as stipulated in Article 23 of the Agreement (https://www.tralac.org/resources/by-region/cfta.html#ratification). The Nigerian government was, for a long time, reluctant to support regional trade liberalization for fear of domestic opposition. Some Nigerians expressed concern that the country could be flooded with low-priced goods, which would impede the development of local manufacturing and farming industries. As the sub-region's largest economy, Nigeria's participation in the free trade area is critical for its success.

The AfCFTA Agreement acknowledges existing regional economic communities "as building blocks towards the establishment of AfCFTA". Within the ECOWAS area, AfCFTA added an additional layer to existing regional trade agreements (http://www.west-africa-brief.org/content/en/west-africa-african-continental-free-trade-area International Journal of Economics and Finance; Vol. 4, No. 10; 2012). The ECOWAS area has the largest number of legal agreements, including the ECOWAS Protocol on the Free Movement of Persons and Goods (1978) and the ECOWAS

Trade Liberalization Scheme (ETLS - 1979), the main operational tool for promoting West Africa as a free trade area. However, in practice, it has been challenging to implement these agreements. AfCFTA will mainly change the relationship between ECOWAS member countries and non-member countries. In line with the AU's Agenda 2063, the role of AfCFTA is to liberalize trade among all African countries. According to the 2017 estimates, intra-regional trade in Africa accounted for only 17% of exports, compare to 59% in Asia and 69% in Europe. However, these figures do not reflect the large amount of informal trade within Africa. AfCFTA presents an opportunity to deepen economic integration beyond West Africa (http://www.west-africa-brief.org/content/en/west-africa-african-continental-free-trade-area) International Journal of Economics and Finance; Vol. 4, No. 10; 2012).

2.3.2. Regional Trade Blocs

There are lots of regional and sub-regional trading intergovernmental organizations in Africa. However, because of their relevance and their past and present experiences, the study has reviewed the EAC, SADC, and ECOWAS. The review of EAC and SADC has shown some similarities with ECOWAS in terms of trade policies and challenges in dealing with the Non-tariff Barriers.

2.3.3. East African Community (EAC)

Historically, cooperation in East Africa, between Kenya, Uganda and Tanzania, goes back a long way on account of these countries being neighbors, their people engaging in trade across the borders, and on having a shared common colonial administration under the British (Mwasha, 2007 pp. 69-70). These countries in 1967 established the East African Community (EAC) which lasted until 1977 when it collapsed for different reasons, including different political ideologies. The Treaty for the establishment of the new "East African Community" was signed by the Heads of State of the partner states on November 30, 1999 in Arusha, Tanzania and came into force on 7th July 2000. The East African Community was formally and officially launched by the Heads of State on 15th January 2001. Rwanda and Burundi joined the EAC in 2007.

The regional co-operation and integration envisaged in the EAC was broad based (Mwasha, 2007 p. 70), covering trade, investments and industrial development; monetary and fiscal affairs; infrastructure and services; human resources, science and technology; agriculture and food security; environment and natural resources management; tourism and wildlife management; and health, social and cultural activities. Further, the EAC offers many benefits to its partner states, including: increased trade, expanded markets, attracting Foreign Direct Investment (FDI), increased bargaining power, strengthening security and resolving conflict as well as ensuring (Mwashi, 2007, p. 69) free movement of people across the region. Further, the EAC member countries undertake several projects together, including transport and communication projects, collective employment and poverty reduction, joint environmental conservation, especially on Lake Victoria, and joint tourism promotion. However, in view of contemporary global trend in which trade negotiations are increasingly being conducted under regional arrangements, and in order to benefit more from integration, strengthening integration (Mwashi, 2007 p.69), ensuring political commitment, good governance, as well as solving the problem of multiple membership facing the region, facilitating trade and solving the problem of Non-tariff Barriers are necessary conditions for success.

2.3.4. Southern African Development Community (SADC)

The main inspiration for regional integration is the political and economic preferences among the members. Regional economic groups eliminate or reduce trade tariffs (and other trade barriers) (Keane, Cali & Kennan, 2010, p. vi) among the member states while maintaining tariffs or barriers for the rest of the world (non-member countries). The lowest level of collaboration in regional arrangements, by and large, involves at least trade, but deeper integration goes further and covers issues other than trade. The SADC with a membership of 15 countries was originally conceived as a bulk mark against apartheid South Africa, by extension, Southern African Countries Union (SACU). The members of SADC are Lesotho, Namibia, South Africa, Botswana, Swaziland, Angola, Democratic Republic of Congo, Madagascar, Malawi, Mauritius, Mozambique, Seychelles, Tanzania, Zambia and Zimbabwe,

The SADC Trade Protocol was designed to reduce or eliminate barriers to trade within the region. NTBs are defined under the SADC Trade Protocol (1996), implemented in 2000, as 'any barrier to trade other than import and export duties. Under the Trade Protocol and Article 6, SADC's position on NTBs is further elaborated with regard to intra-SADC trade: "Except as provided for in this Protocol, Member States shall, in relation to intra-SADC trade (Keane, Cali & Kennan, 2010, p. 10), (a) adopt policies and implement measures to eliminate all existing forms of NTBs; and (b) refrain from imposing any new NTBs".

In support of the SADC Free Trade Area (FTA) launched in August 2008, the following were to be implemented (Keane, Cali & Kennan, 2010, p. 27): (1) gradual elimination of tariffs; (2) adoption of common rules of origin; (3) harmonization of customs rules and procedures; (4) attainment of internationally acceptable standards, quality, accreditation and metrology; (5). harmonization of SPS measures; (6) elimination of NTBs; (7) liberalization of trade in services; and (8) evaluation of trade policies and strategies.

2.3.5. The Economic Community of West African States (ECOWAS)

The Treaty establishing ECOWAS was signed in Lagos, Nigeria on May 28,1975 by the Heads of State and Governments of fourteen (14) West African Countries, namely, Benin, Burkina

Faso, Cote d'Ivoire, Gambia, Ghana, Guinea, Liberia, Mali, Mauritania, Niger, Nigeria, Senegal, Sierra Leone and Togo. Guinea Bissau acceded to the Treaty later in 1975. In 1979, Cape Verde became the 16th member nation. In accordance with its terms, the treaty came into force in June 1975 with the ratification by seven states (Essien, 2006, p. 2). Article 2(1) of the 1975 Treaty describes the aims of ECOWAS as follows:

"… to promote co-operation and development in all fields of economic activity, particularly in the fields of industry, transport, telecommunications, energy, agriculture, natural resources, commerce, monetary and financial questions and in social and cultural matters for the purpose of raising the standard of living of its peoples, of increasing and maintaining economic stability, of fostering closer relations among its members and of contributing to the progress and development of the African continent"

Article2(2) of this Treaty explains that the Community shall, by stages (Essien, pp2-3), ensure:

"(a) the elimination as between the Member States of customs duties and other charges of equivalent effect in respect of the importation and exportation of goods;

(b) the abolition of quantitative and administrative restrictions on trade among the Member States;

(c) the establishment of a common customs tariff and a common commercial policy towards third countries;

(d) the abolition as between the Member States of the obstacles to the free movement of persons, services and capital;

(e) the harmonization of the agricultural policies and the promotion of common projects in the Member States, notably in the fields of marketing, research and afro-industrial enterprises;

(f) the implementation of schemes for the joint development of transport, communication, energy and infrastructure facilities as well as the evolution of a common policy in these fields;

(g) the harmonization of the economic and industrial policies of the Member States and the elimination of disparities in the level of development of Member States;

(h) the harmonization, required for the proper functioning of the Community, of the monetary policies of the Member States;

(i) the establishment of a Fund for Co-operation, Compensation and Development; and

(j) such of the activities calculated to further the aims of the Community"

2.3.6. ECOWAS Trade Liberalization Scheme

From its inception with the signing of the treaty on May 28, 1975 in Lagos, Nigeria, ECOWAS' trade policy has been designed to increase intra-regional commerce, raise trade volume and generally galvanize the economic activities within the region (Essien 2006, p 2) in such a way as to positively impact on the economic wellbeing of citizens of ECOWAS member states. The ECOWAS trade policy is also meant to foster the smooth integration of the region into the world economy with due regard for the political choices and development priorities of states with the desire to engender sustainable development and reduction of poverty.

The main tool of the Community's trade policy is the ECOWAS Trade Liberalization Scheme (ETLS). The scheme was adopted in 1979. The objective of the scheme is to progressively establish a Customs Union among the member states of the Community. The Customs Union will, among others, evolve the total elimination of custom (Essien 2006, pp2-3); (Fajana 2018, p.vi) duties and taxes of equivalent effect. The ETLS covers three groups of products, i.e., unprocessed goods, traditional handicraft products and industrial products.

According to the ECOWAS' Secretariat, the ETLS is meant to give several advantages to citizens of ECOWAS member states ((https://www.ecowas.int/ecowas-sectors/trade/) as they trade among themselves. Some of the advantages accruing to unprocessed goods imported from a member state as contained in Decision C/DEC.8 /11/79 of the Council of Ministers is total exemption from import duties and taxes, free movement without any quantitative restriction as well as non-payment of compensation for loss of revenue as a result of their imports; provided that unprocessed products, among other conditions, originate from member states of the Community and must appear on the list of products annexed to the decisions liberalizing trade in these products. In effect, this also means that the Member States shall not impose new duties and taxes of equivalent effect or increase existing ones (https://www. ecowas.int/ecowas-sectors/trade/). The rates of these duties and taxes which serve as the starting point for the elimination of tariffs are listed in the ECOWAS Customs Tariff for each member state. It is a rule binding on States that there shall be no creation of Non-tariff Barriers and those in existence shall not be increased. Further, the aspect of trade facilitation is an important part of ECOWAS' functions. Trade facilitation involves private sector promotion; the establishment of ECOWAS Common Investment Market, the development of Common Investment Code and Policy, as well as the Ecobiz (trade certification)/ World Market Information System and E-commerce.

2.3.7. ECOWAS Common External Tariff (CET)

The ECOWAS' CET which was launched in 2015 stipulates that there will exist within ECOWAS member states a uniform tariff for all goods imported from non-ECOWAS Countries (https:// www. ecowas.int/ecowas-sectors/trade/).The CET is an important milestone in the creation of a customs union for West Africa.

2.3.8. ECOWAS Regional Agriculture Trade Policy and Institutions

ECOWAS has a comprehensive agriculture trade policy framework with the objective of improving coordination and increasing trade integration between its members. In 2006, ECOWAS agreed with the existing West African Economic and Monetary Union (UEMOA) common external tariff (CET) and the fifth tariff ban at 35 percent was added in 2009 at the behest of Nigeria (Engel and Jouanjean 2013, p.3). However, the CET has not yet been adopted throughout the ECOWAS region. In practice, many countries see the CET as providing insufficient protection for strategic priority commodities, driving unpredictable tariff and non-tariff barriers.

ECOWAS has prioritized food security as a policy objective. ECOWAS adopted an agriculture policy (ECOWAP) in 2005 (Engel and Jouanjean 2013, p.3) with the main objective of boosting agricultural production and exports; attaining food security in member states and promoting sustainable livelihood for farmers. However, the implementation has been largely limited to putting in place instruments and regulations with little analysis thus far to examine the level of implementation and impact. Along the same vein, some trade experts argued that regional agriculture trade policy in West Africa is often just "a patch work of rules" implemented unevenly and enforced inconsistently leading (Engel and Jouanjean, 2013, p.3) to an opaque business environment that limits economic growth potential that agriculture possesses and significantly affect competitive access to food.

Analyzing regional trade flow within West Africa is challenging. Not only that trade flow is poorly reported, with inconsistencies, but also a large amount of trade occurs informally, and therefore it is not recorded in partial databases (Engel and Jouanjean, 2013, p.6); the difference between absence declared and absence trade flow is high, especially trade flow in livestock, onion and coasu grain (millet, sorghum, maize) and rice along selected corridor linking Benin, Burkina Faso, Core D"Ivoire, Ghana, Mali, Niger, Nigeria, Senegal and Togo. The actual trade flow is greater and more diverse than generally recorded.

The key drivers to trade in food staples in West Africa (Engel and Jouanjean, 2013, p.6) have been documented as follows: (a) urbanization as a driver of trade in West Africa, (b) rising income in the region, (c) demand for variety, (d) increasing demand for meat, poultry and dairy products, and (e) population growth and increasing demand for food.

There are many challenges and constraints facing the implementation of the ETLS (Fajana, 2018 p. vii), which have limited its effectiveness and impact as a tool of market integration in West Africa. These challenges include:

1. Lack of domestication of the ETLS at national levels, and the disconnect between the adoption of policies at the regional level and implementation at the national level;
2. Inadequacy of awareness and sensitization on the ETLS in member states;
3. Lack of trust in some member states in the transparency of the process in determining product eligibility and issuing of certificate of origin under the ETLS;
4. Over dependence on import duties by member states for government revenue, and their reluctance to forgo such revenue (And the lack of compensation mechanism for loss of revenue as a result of the implementation of the ETLS);
5. Prevalence of non-tariff barriers that hinder the entry of products in spite of their duty-free status;
6. Inadequate productive capacity, trade-related infrastructure and trade information;
7. Absence of effective mechanism for monitoring and evaluating the implementation of the ETLS, as well as a legal framework for settlement of disputes and enforcement of rights and obligations; and
8. Capacity deficiencies (both institutional and technical) of the ECOWAS Commission.

The estimated total trade of the ECOWAS Region has been put at over $200 billion. The main active countries in trade are Nigeria, which alone accounts for approximately 76 percent of total trade, followed by Ghana (9.2 percent) and Côte d'Ivoire (8.64 percent) (https://www.ecowas.int/ecowas-sectors/trade/). It is dominated by mining commodities (oil resources, iron, bauxite, manganese, gold, etc..) and agriculture (coffee, cocoa, cotton, rubber, fruits and vegetables, and other products rather marketed within the region (dry cereals, roots and tubers, livestock products). Nigeria, Côte d'Ivoire, Ghana and Senegal account for 87 percent of intra-regional trade, with 79 percent of imports and 94 percent of exports and re-exports (https://www.ecowas.int/ecowas-sectors/trade/).

2.4 Nigeria and Liberia Trade Policies

2.4.1. Nigeria Trade Policy

Nigeria's trade policies are discussed under two broad regimes, that is, the period before the introduction of the structural adjustment program (SAP) and the period after its adoption (Analogbei, 2012 p.157). Throughout these regimes, trade policies were short-term in nature and directed at meeting specific objectives, such as ensuring balance of payments viability and export promotion. The trade policies were also meant to complement other policy initiatives, such as, industrialization policy, employment creation and self-sufficiency policies, etc. (Analogbei, 2012 pp. 159-160). The trade policies implemented under the two regimes were as follows:

2.4.2. Pre-SAP Trade Policies (restrictive trade policies)

At independence, Nigeria's economy was in many respects, rural and agrarian (Tamuno and Edoumiekumo, 2012 p. 157), with very narrow industrial base. In an effort to modernize the economy, the early political leaders adopted a development planning strategy (Analogbei, 2012 p. 160) as an instrument for securing a steady and rapid growth of the economy. Emphasis was placed on accelerated development of the economy through expansion in the industrial base. The objective was to produce some consumables locally and, in effect, reduce dependence on external sources for the supply of such goods. In this connection, the emphasis of trade policies was on production for export of cash crops in order to expand industrialization. The export of cash crops was then the main source of foreign exchange. Thus, farmers were encouraged to expand their production of cash crops (Analogbei, 2012, p. 160) with guaranteed external markets by the marketing boards. The export basket consisted of cocoa, palm produce, rubber, groundnut, ginger and some solid minerals, coal and tin. The insatiable urge to quicken the drive for development gave rise to heightened demand for imports (Analogbei, 2012. P. 160), which in turn exerted pressures on the balance of payments.

Also, in order to give effect to the import substitution industrialization policy, trade barrier in the form of imports licensing was put in place to complement imports tariffs in the control of imports, as well as protect domestic industries that were set up to produce import substitutes. The customs tariff structure was deliberately discriminatory (Analogbei, 2012 p161), biased in favour of capital goods and raw materials. Items considered as luxury goods were either put on import prohibition list or had very high import tariffs placed on them. In terms of directional flow of trade, Nigeria's imports and exports were concentrated in Europe, Asia and the Americas due to historical inheritance. After the end of the Nigerian civil war, Nigeria's major economic strategy was to secure economic growth through the replacement of destroyed assets and restoration of the productive capacity of the country. It was also envisaged that by the end of the plan period (1970-74) (Analogbei, 2012. P.160), Nigeria would have been able to produce its own goods and services, finance development, and enjoy favorable balance of trade. Towards this end, the plan was designed to enhance agricultural and industrial production, as well as high and intermediate level manpower (Analogbei, 2012 p. 161). In order to reduce the pressure on imports, restrictive trade policies were strengthened; exchange control measures and import licensing were intensified, as well as increasing number of non-essential imports were placed under ban.

Further, some finished consumer products considered not essential were placed under specific license (Analogbei, 2012 p.161) so as to keep their importation within specified quota. Due to the sudden and unexpected increase in the prices of crude petroleum in 1973, coupled with the country's low absorptive capacity (Analogbei, 2012 p. 162) and the existence of various production bottlenecks in the economy, the exchange control regulations needed to be liberalized. Consequently, the restrictions on import payments were removed in 1974 (Analogbei, 2012 p.162).

The restrictive trade policies were accordingly relaxed following the boom from the crude oil export earnings. By 1985, the Nigerian economy had started experiencing decline in foreign exchange earnings and oil shock. Oil price fell sharply, while the demand for imports continued to surge. The imports demand became price inelastic (Analogbei, 2012 p. 162), thus causing balance of payments deficit. Concerted efforts were then made to control the import trend through the imposition of stricter trade restrictions. The high level of controls further created administrative bottlenecks. The inability of the control measures (Analogbei, 2012 p. 162) to effectively secure downward adjustment to imports demand against the backdrop of falling export earnings gave rise to serious payments imbalances.

2.4.3. Trade Policies During SAP

In July 1986, the Structural Adjustment Program (SAP) was introduced to tackle the restrictive trade policies of the pre-SAP era, which caused the imbalances in the economy. The main elements (Analogbei, 2012 p. 163) of the program included (a) restructure and diversify the productive base of the economy in order to lessen the dependence on the oil sector and on imports; (b) achieve fiscal and balance of payments viability over time; (c) lay the basis for sustainable, non-inflationary growth; and (d) lessen the dominance of unproductive investments in the public sector, improve the sector's efficiency and intensify the growth potential of the private sector.

During the SAP era, the trade policy was on the side of liberalization. Relative to international trade, the primary focus was on liberalization of trade and the pricing system (Analogbei, 2012 p.

163); emphasis was on the use of appropriate price mechanism for the allocation of foreign exchange. The Second-tier Foreign Exchange Market (SFEM) was then introduced, under which the exchange rate of the naira to the US dollar was to be determined by the market forces of demand and supply (Analogbei, 2012. P. 163). It became clear that trade openness has a significant impact on economic growth; trade openness made sense in Nigeria, and there is a causal relationship between economic growth and trade openness (Kalu and Agodi, 2015 p. 6).

Therefore, the application of import and export licensing was unnecessary, and consequently abolished. Further, to encourage export activities, the policy which required exporters to surrender their export proceeds to the Central Bank of Nigeria, was abolished. As such, exporters were allowed to retain 100 percent of their export earnings (Analogbei, 2012 p.163) in their domiciliary accounts from where they could freely draw to meet all eligible foreign exchange transactions. Further, under the revised duty drawback/suspension scheme, exporters/producers could import raw materials and intermediate products free from imports duty (Analogbei, 2012 p. 163) and other indirect taxes and charges. The Export Incentive and Miscellaneous Provisions Decree of 1986 was promulgated to encourage exports.

Also, the Nigerian Export Credit Guarantee and Insurance Corporation came on stream in 1988, and was subsequently renamed Nigerian Export-Import Bank (NEXIM), to provide credit and risk bearing facilities to banks (Analogbei, 2012 p. 163) so as to encourage them to support exports. In the area of imports, the devalued exchange rate of the naira at the different shades of the foreign exchange market was meant to make imports dearer, thus discourage importation and reduce the pressure on balance of payments. Import licensing was abolished and reliance was placed on the use of customs tariff for the control of imports. The list of items on the imports prohibition list was also drastically reduced (Analogbei, 2012 p.164). As such, Nigeria witnessed a sharp rise in the volume and value of trade with other nations of the world.

Foreign trade statistics, according to Economic Intelligence Unit (EIU) Country Report of 2009 (Oluwasola Omoju & Olumide

Adesanya, 2012), pp.743-755) revealed that in 2007, total export was valued at $61.8 billion (free on board), while import was valued of $38.7 billion (free on board). Further breakdown of the composition of imports and exports showed that fuel and mining products, agricultural products, and manufactures accounted for 97%, 2.2% and 0.8% of total exports, respectively; while machinery, agricultural products, and fuel and mining products accounted for 72.3%, 23.7% and 4% of total imports, respectively. According to statistics released by the National Bureau of Statistics, Nigeria's total trade figure for the second quarter of 2009 was N2,210.3 trillion. Though, this figure reflects a decline of 37.9 % when compared with the corresponding period in 2008; it indicates an increase of 11.9% over that of the first quarter of 2009. This trend was expected over the long term due to increased trade liberalization to foster economic growth across the world.

Nonetheless, bulk of Nigeria's trade goes to Europe, Asia and the Americas (see Table 1 below); only Ghana made it on the list of the first 10 countries of Nigeria's export trade destination.

Table 1 - Nigeria's Trade Destination (1st Quarter 2019))

No. Rank	Country	% Share of Exports	No. Rank	Country	% Share of Imports
1	India	16.43%	1.	China	28%
2	Spain	10.7%	2.	Swaziland	14.28%
3.	Nethelands	8.9%	3	USA	8.7%
4.	South Africa	7.2%	4	India	6.55%
5.	France	6.6%	5	The Netherlands	4.07%
6	Angola	4.47%	6.	Belgium	3.37%
7.	Italy	3.96%	7.	Germany	3.52%
8.	Turkey	3.96%	8.	United Kingdom	2.57%
9.	Ghana	3.43%	9.	Italy	2.39%
10.	Sweden	3.33%	10.	South Africa	1.72%

Source: https://nairametrics.com/2019/08/12/top-trading-partners-for-nigerias-exports-and-imports-in-2019/

2.4.4. Liberia's Trade Policy

Liberia's trade policy over the years has been a policy to attract foreign investors through the "Open Door Policy", where investors were allowed to repatriate their profits one hundred percent (100%). In latter days, Liberia's trade policy included liberalization through ECOWAS and WTO trade protocols and rules. The first section deals with Liberia's Open-Door Policy, while the second section discusses Liberia's current trade policy, the Liberia National Trade Policy (a trade liberalization policy).

2.4.5. Liberia's Open-Door Policy (Initial Trade and Investment Policy)

The Open-Door Policy was the principal trade policy for Liberia from the early 1920's to the 1960s. The decision of President Edwin Barclay (1930-1944) to adopt the US dollar as the sole legal tender in Liberia as of December 31,1943 symbolized his Administration's desire to open up the country for foreign capital. Immediately after being inaugurated as President King's successor, Mr. Edwin Barclay further "opened the door" that for so long, since 1864, had been closed (Kaaij 1983) for foreign investors and traders. Mr. Barclay's predecessor, President Charles D. B. King already had agreed with the Firestone Rubber Plantation Company to come to Liberia in 1926. After having been duly elected in 1931, President Edwin Barclay stated in his first Inaugural Address in January 1932 that "We shall encourage the investment of productive foreign capital". "We can only save and develop our hinterland by the help of the European trader", including white Americans in this group as well (Kaaij, 1983).

One of the first official decisions of President Edwin Barclay was to repeal the famous Port of Entry Law of 1864 (Kaaij 1983) that restricted the economic activities of foreigners in the country. Subsequently, in the early 1930s, concession agreements were signed between the Liberian Government and the Dutch,

Danish, German and Polish Investors. Significantly, in 1937 President Barclay, after pressure from the USA, withdrew the concession agreement with the German Investors, (Kaaij 1983) who were accused of sympathizing with the Nazi Regime in their home country.

During the first quarter of the 20th century, both the British and American currencies freely circulated in Liberia as legal tender. The arrival of the Firestone Rubber Plantation Company in 1926 enhanced the importance of the American dollar since the US company (Kaaij 1983), the largest employer in the country, paid its employees in US dollars. But the arrival of the Firestone Rubber Plantation Company brought more changes, notably as a result of the US$5 million loan that accompanied the United States' investment.

Furthermore, during World War II, in 1942, the United States government obtained a military base in Liberia, and later it granted a loan to Liberia with the proceeds of which the Free Port of Monrovia was constructed (Kaaij 1983) and a railway built, connecting Liberia's first iron ore mine at Bomi Hills with the Free Port of Monrovia. Thus, when, in December 1943, President Edwin Barclay decided to outlaw the British pound and to make the US dollar the only legal tender in the country, it was a logical decision that confirmed the political orientation of the country, as well as its financial and economic dependence on the United States government.

The decision paid well as was demonstrated by the arrival of United States Investors (Kaaij, 1983), including Messr. Lansdell Christie and Edward R. Stettinius. Mr. Lansdell Christie, a former Colonel in the United States Army, who, during World War II served in Liberia and became acquainted with the country and its economic potential, started Liberia's first modern iron ore mine with the establishment of the Liberian Mining Company, in 1945 (Kaaij 1983). Similarly, Mr. Edward R. Stettinius had become familiar with Liberia during his official duties as US Secretary of State. After his retirement, in 1947, he concluded a major concession agreement with the Liberian Government (Kaaij, 1983), resulting in the establishment of the Liberian Mining Company, and influenced the launching of Liberia's flag-of-convenience policy. Many other investors from the USA, Sweden, the Netherlands and Germany followed. All this happened during the Administration of President William V. S. Tubman to whom Liberia's Open Door Policy is usually attributed. The Liberian Government shared less in the profits of foreign investments (Kaaij 1983) than it had initially thought. As an incentive to attract foreign investors, the government of Liberia offered (Kaaij 1983): (i) long tax holidays, (ii) long exemption period of import and export duties, (iii) special tax tariffs for some investors and (iv) many and large tax-deductible items in cases where investors are liable to taxes.

2.4.6. The Liberia National Trade Policy (Current trade policy)

The current trade policy of Liberia is summarized in the Act establishing the Ministry of Commerce and Industry (MoCI). The Ministry is the principal arm of the Government of Liberia (GoL) responsible for managing trade and commerce of Liberia. Section 651 of the Act establishing the MoCI (1987) states the functions of the Ministry (GoL, Ministry of Commerce and Industry Annual Report, 2016, pp. 9-10), inter alia, as follows: the promotion, development, regulation, and the control, operation and expansion of commercial, industrial enterprises and activities in the Republic. Further, the Ministry shall exercise broad powers with respect to and protection of public interest and the achievement of national goals, through the establishment and enforcement of standards for commodities and trade. In further execution of its functions, the MoCI shall also do the following:

(a) Establish and regulate commodity and trade standards;

(b) Collect, evaluate, and publish data pertaining to commerce and industry;

(c) Establish and enforce standards of business practice;

(d) Promote sound and development of foreign and domestic commerce;

(e) Develop plans for the movements of goods and people within and without the Republic; and

(f) Perform such other function as may be assigned from time to time by the president of Liberia.

2.4.7. The Liberia National Trade Policy Objectives

In pursuance of its policy objectives, the government of Liberia adopted a more comprehensive trade objective of enhancing trade liberalization, and acceding to ECOWAS trade protocols and schemes, and WTO rules. The overall objective of the Liberia National Trade Policy (LNTP) (2014 – 2019) is to promote international trade (exports and imports) and to engender a more competitive domestic private sector by supporting the agricultural, industrial and service sectors (Liberia National Trade Policy, 2014, p. 5). In this way, trade will be contributing to employment generation, improvement of livelihood, and reduction in poverty. Further, the LNTP also has the following objectives: to promote a balanced relationship between trade integration and sustainable development; contribute to a more transparent and predictable business environment, and protect both domestic businesses as well as the disadvantaged (Liberia National Trade Policy, 2014 – 2019, p. 5), including women, youth and the poor (especially those living in rural areas), from the adverse effect of market opening:

The key policy areas of the Liberia National Trade Policy (2014 – 2019) (LNTP 2014, pp.6-7) are as follows:

1. Promotion of international trade: to promote international export competitiveness through a variety of actions ranging from infrastructure to export incentives. At present, Liberia's trade related economic infrastructure, such as road and rail networks, power and electricity, telecommunication network, and other facilities, is largely inadequate, which increases the cost of production and distribution of goods and services

domestically, regionally and internationally. The availability of appropriately high-quality infrastructure improves turn-around time, reduces prices, and improves the efficiency of delivery. Therefore, the LNTP is designed to address problems related to export incentives, trade promotion, economic infrastructure and services. The infrastructure include transport, electricity, telecommunications, internet, trade finance, and sector-specific issues.

2. Promotion of domestic trade: to promote domestic trade and strengthen the productive capacity in order for more businesses to become export ready. In addition, the trade policy objective is to ensure an efficiently functioning domestic market, thus ensuring the production of competitive products through the forces of demand and supply. The objective is also to foster productivity through competition, thereby establishing the basis for increased exports through the creation of productive export-ready businesses. The LNTP strategy therefore is to support Liberian producers and traders by improving the business environment and specific support at the firm level. The targeted areas of the national trade policy are improvement of domestic trade infrastructure, assistance to indigenous producers and traders, protection and strengthening of intellectual property rights, and facilitation of access to finance and land.

3. Trade facilitation: to increase the efficiency of import and export administration and trade facilitation. Effective trade facilitation can have a significant impact on economic development, contribute to export growth, and improve the competitiveness of Liberian goods and services on the global market. Further, effective trade facilitation can contribute to improving customs services for enhanced revenue collection and regulatory control. Thus, improved border and transit infrastructure is an important component of the trade facilitation strategy.

4. Promotion of trade within ECOWAS and the Manu River Union (MRU): to promote regional trade and integration, primarily in the context of the MRU and ECOWAS. The objective of this policy area is to create a larger market for Liberian products. ECOWAS, as a full customs union, provides a larger market and increases the potential for industrialization and investment. In Liberia, regional cross border trade (both small and large scale) is on the rise for both rural and urban traders. However, tariff and non-tariff barriers still exist and make regional trade a challenge for cross border traders. In order to support regional integration, the LNTP addresses the implementation of the ECOWAS Trade Liberalization Scheme (ETLS) and Common External Tariff (CET), the progressive reduction of regional non-tariff measures and trade-related issues, and the promotion of wider trade integration.

5. Global market access: to promote global market access for Liberian goods and services through WTO membership and the efficient use of preferential trade agreements and preference schemes. Under this policy area, Liberia will diversify its exports and pursue industrialization as well as broaden exports to regional and international markets. In order to achieve this policy objective, the policy espoused a three-pronged strategy: (a) through Liberia's accession to and active participation in the WTO; (b) maximizing the benefits from market access and technical assistance under the EU/Liberia Economic Partnership Agreement; and (c) proactively using preferential trade agreements and preference schemes.

Other policy areas encompass institutional strengthening, capacity building, and good governance in the administration of the trade policy. The Liberia National Trade Policy acknowledges the need for institutional strengthening of relevant trade facilitation institutions (Liberia National Trade Policy 2014 – 2019, pp.12-13), such as the Ministry of Commerce and Industry, the National Standard Laboratory (NSL), and the trade statistics database. And at the legal and governance levels, the LNTP espouses guaranteeing transparency and predictability of trade rules in Liberia, ensuring fair competition and consumer protection, and building capacity for effective resolution of trade disputes.

2.4.8. Liberia and the World Trade Organization

In July 2016, Liberia joined the World Trade Organization (WTO) as its 163rd member after successful completion of negotiation on one market access. Liberia's membership was approved on Dec 10, 2015 at the 10th Ministerial Conference held in Nairobi, Kenya (MoCI Annual Report 2016, Foreword). The benefits of joining the WTO (MoCI Annual Report 2017 Annex 1 – p. 37) include the following: (a) Access to Most Favor Nation tariff rates; National Treatment of Liberian goods in other members' markets, access to dispute settlement, the opportunity to attract investment; (b) increased awareness of the gains from trade, visibility and credibility with trading partners, and (c) the adoption of rules and regulations that respect the principles of non-discrimination and national treatment

As part of Liberia's WTO Accession Plan activities, the government of Liberia (GoL) in collaboration with the International Trade Corporation (ITC), launched the Tourism Strategy, Tourism Website, and made progress in the development of the Kpatawee Waterfall (MoCI Annual Report 2016 - Foreword). Further, Liberia streamlined the Import licensing requirements in line with the WTO Agreement on Import Licensing Procedures and the need to improve on trade policy indicator under the Millennium Challenge Corporation (MCC) Program. The MoCI reduced the number of product categories requiring Import Permit Declaration (IPD) from seventeen (17) to eleven (11) (MoCI Annual Report 2016 - Foreword). The core products requiring IPDs were restricted to mainly consumables, to protect the health of consumers. (MoCI Annual Report 2016 -Foreword). And the Legislature enacted and ratified the Intellectual Property (IP) Law, the Liberia WTO Accession Protocol and the World Intellectual Property Organization (WIPO) instruments (Conventions, Treaties and Protocols).

Further, the government of Liberia made progress since the country accession to the WTO in 2016 (MoCI 2016 pp.12-13) in the following areas: (1) launching the post accession plan, (2) forging multinational trade integration (Liberia's participation in three rounds of the Continental Free Trade Area for the establishment of free trade areas among member states), (3) development of a national export strategy; (4) development of Rubber Wood Furniture Strategy (5) passage of the Foreign Trade Competition and Intellectual Property Laws; (6) Procurement Law, (7) adoption of International Standards on SPS, (8) Quality Policy in order to enhance trade facilitation as part of the West Africa Quality System Program, and (9) regulatory framework for the production of liquefied petroleum gas, wheat flour, packages (sachet) water droplets in Liberia.

2.4.9. Meeting Sanitary and Phyto-Sanitary Requirement under the World Trade Organization (WTO)

Meeting WTO standards for exportation of plants and animal products require, inter alia, certification of a responsible national institution, i.e., the National Standard Laboratory (NSL). One key constraint affecting Liberia's trade regime is the lack of quality laboratory for testing and calibration of imports in keeping with the World Health Organization (WHO) regulations. The NSL was established as a testing and calibration facility (MoCI Annual Report, 2017 p.23), and linked to the country's initiative and processes to meeting WTO regulations on Sanitary and Phytosanitary (SPS) requirements. The NSL was set-up in 2011 so as to prevent the importation of sub-standard products that would threaten public, plant or animal health, and for assuring that food and agriculture exports from Liberia meet international standards.

The NSL has three major laboratories (MoCI Annual Report 2017, p. 23) aimed at testing imported goods and calibrating equipment, namely: (1) the Chemical Testing Laboratory, which provides analytical testing services for the purpose of determining whether foods meet specification in order to protect consumers' interest, and to verify claims on labels, (2) the Microbiology Laboratory, which provides microbiological testing services for the purpose of protecting consumes' economic interest, verifies producers' claims, and ensures that products do not contain microbial contaminations, and (3) the Metrology Laboratory, which provides calibration services to businesses and laboratories, thereby ensuring that customers receive a fair value for their money spent. The problem however remains that the NSL has not gotten international certification.

2.4.10. Liberia and ECOWAS

Liberia is a founding member of the Economic Community of West African States (ECOWAS) (1975). ECOWAS' main objective is to create a customs union, a free trade area. Like other regional blocs, such as the SADC, the key tenets of ECOWAS regional trade objectives (MoCI Annual Report 2017, p. 30) are: (1) Abolition of customs duties on imports and exports of ECOWAS' locally produced goods; (2) Liberalization of trade throughout ECOWAS member countries to create a common market; (3) Removal of Non-tariff Barriers; and (4) Regional protection of ECOWAS' produced goods. However, the implementation of the ECOWAS Trade Liberalization Scheme and the Common External Tariff by member states, including Liberia has been very slow.

In 2010, ECOWAS adopted the "West African Common Industrial Policy" with the objective of increasing the share of intra-regional trade to 40% by 2030 (MoCI Annual Report 2017, p.30). This is the latest step in a long history of attempts at regional integration in West Africa. With its small domestic market size, Liberia's takeoff depends on regional trade, which will open up export market opportunities.

In this way, Liberia can tap into ECOWAS' $4.6bn per year fish market, $2bn cooking oils and soaps market, and $360m non-tire rubber products market (MoCI Annual Report 2017, p.30). Also, Liberia is gradually adopting ECOWAS' CET, which will be beneficial to the country by allowing for deeper integration and strengthening economic cooperation in the region. However, the implementation of the CET by Liberia is being held back because of the tariff rates. The goal of ECOWAS was to pursue full compliance with the CET rates by 2020 (this was not achieved). The government of Liberia's concern about the implementation of the CET is that moving the average tariff from 5.3% to 13% will result to higher costs for consumers (MoCI Annual Report 2017, p. 30). The implementation of the CET will also lead to reduction in imports by 3.8%, and the economy will experience higher prices for imports.

Along with the CET, Liberia is promoting regional trade through the implementation of the ECOWAS Trade Liberalization Scheme (ETLS). Under the ETLS, products produced locally can be traded within ECOWAS free of custom duties; although companies are to apply to the National Approval Committee in order to be permitted to benefit from the ETLS (GoL MoCI Annual Report 2017 p. 30). Liberia has been unable to fully tap into the regional export potentials because the National Standards Laboratory (NSL) has not been certificated or accredited, as meeting international standards. Without an accredited standards laboratory, Liberian exporters won't be qualified to export their products to the international market. The NSL and the Ghana Standards Authority signed a Memorandum of Understanding(MOU) (MoCI Annual Report 2017, p. 30) for technical support to the NSL over the years.

2.4.11. Liberia's Trade Destination

Liberia's current intra-ECOWAS trade is negligible. Like Nigeria, bulk of Liberia's trade is with the Americas. Europe and Asia. Table 2 below shows Liberia's trade destinations, exports and imports. The United States of America gets most of Liberia's exports, 23.8%, followed by South Africa, 19.6%. On the Import front, about 44.9% of Liberia's imports come from Ghana and 9.8% from the USA.

Table 2 – Liberia's Trade Destination (2013)

No Rank.	Country	% Share of Exports	No. Rank	Country	% Share of Imports
1.	USA	23,8%	1.	Ghana	44.9%
2.	South Africa	19.6%	2.	USA	9.8%
3.	Spain	7.7%	3.	France	4.1%
4.	Mozambique	6.1%	4.	Ivory Coast	3.7%
5.	Canada	6.1%	5.	Turkey	3.5%
6.	Denmark	5.6%	6.	The Netherlands	3.1%
7.	Germany	4.3%	7.	India	2.6%
8.	Belgium	4.0%	8.	Thailand	2.1%
9.	The Netherlands	2.8%	9.	Spain	2.1%
10.	India	2.5%	10.	Malaysia	1.5%

Source: Regional and Global Trade Strategy for Liberia, 2013, p.10

2.5 Trade Policy Implementation Constraints and Challenges

All of the preferential schemes under the WTO, and agreements under regional trade organizations, including ECOWAS, are linked to rules of origin and other NTBs. To date, most Liberian business people are unable to export under the preferential trade agreements (MoCI Annual Report 2017, pp. 28-29); only five companies exported under the rules, i.e., one company under Africa Growth

Opportunity Act (AGOA), and four companies under the Mano River Union (MRU).

Additionally, structural bottlenecks continue to hold back Liberia's competitiveness. Trading in Liberia is still severely constrained with very few firms participating in international markets. Liberian businesses are faced with low productivity and higher trade costs (Liberia National Trade Policy, 2014 p. 5) when compared to other countries. Exports are highly concentrated on very few primary products and few market destinations. Liberia's trade capacity for effective participation in global markets is limited, and the quality of goods and services produced domestically is generally low. This is due to low level of technology and lack of value chains. Further, reliable and timely trade statistics are largely absent; and trade skills and negotiation capacity are limited. The cost of doing business in Liberia is still high, and the informal trade sector remains large" (LNTP 2014-2019 p.5). Therefore, in order to achieve the trade policy objectives and gain from increased trade integration, Liberia needs to address a multiple of domestic constraints for firms to invest, produce, and export, including trade regulatory formwork, technical infrastructure (i.e., the NSL, sea port facilities). Although since 2009, some progress has been made in other macroeconomic areas. Nevertheless, improvement of the overall business environment and trade facilitation, including NTBs remain wanting.

2.6 Non-Tariff Barriers: Hurdles to Free Trade within ECOWAS/ Liberia and Nigeria

The NTBs are barriers, other than tariffs, that affect the flow of trade. Some NTBs are caused by non-compliance with national trade rules and /or regional trade agreements. Other NTBs are imposed by national agreements through policies that restrict trade. For example, the nature and extent of NTBs in Agriculture trade in West Africa under the ECOWAS Trade Liberalization Scheme was summarized (Harris Chambers & Foresti (2011 pp3-4) as follows:

(1) Gabs between regional agreements, national legislation, and implementation (which make implementation of regional trade protocols difficult); (2) Limited private sector knowledge about ECOWAS' free trade protocols; (3) Strong incentive for informal trade; (4) Non-functioning inter-state road transit (ISRT) regime (e.g., non-compliance with truck axle load); (5) Non-compliance with the certificate of origin rule; (6) Poor state of seaports facilities; (7) Widespread bribery at check points on the interstate highways; (8) Poor Sanitary and Phytosanitary Standards for animal products; and (9) Inadequate inspection system.

Further, some ECOWAS member states do impose ban on trade in certain commodities even amongst themselves. For example, Ghana would impose bans and restrictions often for months, on unprocessed agricultural products; Burkina Faso would impose seasonal restrictions on maize; while Senegal and Togo would require escort services for transit goods. This, in part, is driven by the pace of liberalization and integration (Harris, Chambers & Foresti, 2011); and the fear of inadequate protection for local producers has caused the proliferation of NTBs in the region.

Also, the pace of multilateral and regional liberalization and the poor state of the maritime/port facilities exacerbate the scale of the NTBs. This creates a "vicious cycle", where exports from West Africa remain weak because of high maritime transport tariff, which induces low traffic and therefore raises tariff even further (https:// www. ecowas.int/ecowas-sectors/trade). Furthermore, one of the overarching problems in this regard is the prevalence of informal practices that exacerbate transport and shipping costs, including the widespread nature of corruption and bribery on trade routes in the region, and the trucking cartels. Therefore, deregulating the trucking industry in West Africa is a necessary condition for a more competitive market. The demand for trucking could be served more efficiently in a liberalized trucking industry. In the area of Sanitary and Phyto-Sanitary Standards (SPS), analysis of the data on the maritime industry points to the poor state of sea ports in ECOWAS member countries as a barrier to trade flow. Also, inadequate inspection system has been identified as a barrier.

There is a need for an integrated strategy to develop testing capacity and eliminate redundancies; and forge greater commitments for regional standardization, harmonization, and participation (https://www.ecowas.int/ecowas-sectors/trade/). It has been further observed that successful regional integration elsewhere in the world highlights the tackling of Non-tariff Barrier as a necessity condition to enhance trade (Engel and Jouanjean 2013 p. 7). The NTBs, whether protectionist interest or not, raise trade costs and inhibit regional trade. Efforts to facilitate trade in the region must aim to address NTBs.

CHAPTER THREE: RESEARCH METHODOLOGY

3.0 Introduction

This Chapter discusses the research method for the study, research design, target population, sample size, and sampling techniques. It also discusses the research instruments, data collection procedures and analysis.

3.1 Research Method

For the purpose of this study, the qualitative research method was used. The qualitative research method encompasses all forms of social inquiries (Flick, 2009, pp. 31-32) that rely primarily on non-numeric data in the form of words, including all types of textual analysis such as content, conversation, discourse and narrative analysis. The aim of qualitative analysis inquiry is to understand the meaning of human action by describing the observations. Qualitative method approach is used mainly for processual studies.

Qualitative research has gained momentum as a mode of inquiry. It is a form of systematic inquiry, i.e., "plan, order and publish" base on rules agreed upon by the qualitative research community. Qualitative research method is of specific relevance to the study of social reforms due to the "pluralization" of the world; the "new obscurity", and the growing "individualization" of ways of living and biographical patterns (Flick 2009, pp. 30, 42).

Generally, the data of qualitative research produce more contextual information about the respondents.

This study assessed the impact of the NTBs on trade flow between Liberia and Nigeria. It is a processual study; it assessed the processes, i.e., "the what, how, and why?" about the trade flow between Liberia and Nigeria, and ECOWAS at large. Which NTBs are responsible for the phenomena, how, and why? The researcher looked for the points of view of the respondents on the effect of NTBs on trade flow; their experiences (successes, challenges and constraints), and their recommendations for reform. The researcher engaged the business people of the Liberia Marketing Association (LMA) (Waterside Branch) to talk about the effects of Non-tariff Barriers on their businesses, e.g., the long customs procedures, high level of corruption at checkpoints, etc. How are the NTBs impacting business flow between Liberia and Nigeria? How are the NTBs affecting the free movement of goods and people in keeping with ECOWAS protocols. And which reform measures should the governments of Liberia and Nigeria execute; and which ECOWAS protocol should be enforced or reformed. The study is contextual and descriptive in its analysis. The research is a probing study in order to understand the problem and identify the solution and recommendations for reform, from those who are directly affected by the abnormality.

3.2 Research Design

For this study, exploratory research design was used by the researcher to study, examine, analyze and investigate the research problem. A research design is a framework of research method and techniques selected by the researcher to undertake the study. A good research design usually creates minimum bias (Bhat 2009) in the data and increases trust in the accuracy of the collected data. There are four key characteristics (Bhat 2009) of a good research design: (1) Neutrality (assumption that the data must be free from bias, and must be neutral), (2) Reliability (the expected result will only be achieved if the result is reliable); (3) Validity (having the necessary tools that will enable the researcher to gauge the result of the study, (i.e., the open-ended questions developed from the design should be valid), and (4) generalization (the outcome of the result should be applied to the target population, not just the sample size).

3.2.1. Exploratory Research Design

As mentioned above, exploratory research design is a broad-ranging, purposive, systematic and pre-arranged undertaking designed to maximize the discovery of generalization (Stebbins, 2011), thus leading to description and understanding of the subject under study. It involves description of facts, concepts, structure arrangements, social pressures and beliefs, etc. Exploratory research contributes to identifying new ideas and insights. By using the exploratory research design, the researcher evaluated underlying causes of the problem. The design enabled the researcher to learn more about the facts, factors and circumstances that restrict trade. The researcher identified the causes and effects of the Non-tariff Barriers on trade flow within the ECOWAS sub-region, and more specifically, between Liberia and Nigeria (our case study). The study investigated the impact of the NTBs on the traders, those ordinary people doing business between Liberia and Nigeria, as well as countries in between (Cote D'Ivoire, Ghana, Togo, and Benin). The researcher reviewed the trade policies of the two countries, as well as ECOWAS protocols and the WTO rules, that for many ECOWAS member countries, have become difficult to implement and therefore limiting trade flow.

3.3 Target Population

For the purpose of this study, the target population was the members of the Liberian Marketing Association (Waterside Branch). The total membership was estimated at 45,000 market men, women and youth. The target population is the total group of people from where a sample (a subset of individuals from a target population) is drawn for the study. A sample is a group of people who take part in the survey or investigation. The first key factor however is generalization, which means the extent to which the findings of the study can be generalized or applied (Lavrakas, 2008) to the target population from where the sample is drawn. In other words, a target population of a survey defines those units for which the findings of the survey are meant to generalize. The target population is the entire set of units from which the sample data are to be used to make inferences.

For the purpose of this study on the impact of NTBs on the flow of trade between Liberia and Nigeria, and ECOWAS at large, the target population was the members of the Liberia Marketing Association (LMA) (Waterside Branch), which has a membership of 45,000 (forty-five thousand) marketers. From the list of the members of the LMA (Waterside Branch), the researcher randomly selected a sample of thirty (30) respondents, who traveled between Liberia and Nigeria on business trips to participate in the study.

3.4 Sample Size and Sampling Techniques

3.4.1. Sample Size

A sample size is a small group of people or units drawn from the target population to be surveyed. The goal of the sample size is to make inferences about the population from the sample. In practice, the sample size selected from the population should have sufficient statistical power. For the purpose of this study, the researcher used a sample size of thirty (30) respondents drawn from the membership of the LMA (Waterside branch) to answer the open-ended questions, and also to participate in the focus group discussion. Of the thirty respondents, 15 provided answers to the open-ended questions, while the other 15 respondents participated in the focus group discussion.

3.4.2. Sampling Techniques

With respect to the sampling techniques, the researchers used the simple random sampling technique to select the sample size for the study. From the membership list that the researcher got from the LMA, a sample was selected, using a simple random sampling technique. In that way, every member of this target population had equal chance of being selected to form part of the sample size for the study.

3.5 Research Instruments

For the purpose of this study, the researcher used a combination of research instruments: self-developed open-ended interview questions, and focused group discussion. A research instrument is a tool use to collect, measure, and analyze data relative to the study. The researcher's instruments could include questionnaires, interviews, tests, or checklists. For the purpose of this study on the impact of NTBs on trade flow between Liberia and Nigeria, the researcher used a combination of research instruments. First, the researcher developed a list of open-ended questions, which was administered to the sample of 15 respondents of the target population. Also, with the cooperation of the respondents, a focus group discussion was held with the second set of 15 respondents, totaling 30 respondents. The second instrument was used for corroboration and to determine the veracity of the answers provided by the first set of respondents, who provided answers to the open-ended questions.

3.6 Data Collection and Analysis Procedures

3.6.1 Data collection procedures

How data is gathered and analyzed depends on many factors, including the context, the issue that needs to be monitored, the purpose of the data collection, and the nature and size of the organization. In the interest of effectiveness and efficiency, it is essential that the data collected should shed light on the issue under study. To protect the credibility and reliability of data, information should be gathered, using accepted data collection techniques.

For the purpose of this study, the researcher developed and administered open-ended interview questions. The instrument gave the respondents the opportunity to share their views, perceptions, and experiences on the issues under study, the impact of the NTBs on trade flow between Liberia and Nigeria. The open-ended interview questions were administered to 15 out of the 30 respondents that were part of the sample size for the study; the second set of 15 respondents participated in the focus group interview/ discussions, where the respondents were allowed to answer the questions freely. The answers were unrestricted and unguided. After developing and pre-testing of the open-ended interview questions, the researchers visited the offices of the LMA (Waterside Branch) and introduced himself and explained the purpose of the visit.

At the introductory meeting, the researcher sought the approval of the leadership of the marketers to conduct the research. The researcher explained that this study was for academic purposes only and stressed the need for their informed consent, meaning that they were not compelled to participate in the study. The researcher answered all the questions that the respondents asked. Thereafter, the researcher requested from the leader for the list of the target population in order to facilitate the application of the random sampling technique in selecting the sample of participants. After the sampling exercise, the researcher went to Waterside on several days to hold the interview with the respondents, asking the questions and writing down the answers. On many occasions, the interview was interrupted in order to allow the respondents to serve customers and then return to continue with the interview. The focus group discussion was held at the market place of the president (the head of the marketers) in the market hall, where they were invited for that purpose.

At the beginning of the interview, the researcher provided an overview of the study and the general research techniques, including the focus group interview. The researcher reminded respondents and ensured that they understood their rights as volunteer participants; that they were free to withdraw at any time if they didn't want to continue with the interview. The researcher also informed them that this study was for academic purposes only.

The data collection process was done through the administration of the open-ended questions to the respondents in the form of an interview. The interview focused mainly on the respondent's experiences, views and perceptions. At the beginning of the interview, the researcher introduced himself, and the respondents did the same. During the focus group discussion, the questions were asked, anyone could answer, and the others could buttress or provide a contrary view. The researcher took notes and later transcribed the data into prose.

3.6.2. Data Analysis Procedures

The data collected from the field was compiled and coded according to the themes of the study. The data from the open-ended questions were analyzed qualitatively and the results presented in prose form. Also, the data collected from the focus group discussions were analyzed and presented in prose form. The researcher was also looking for corroboration in the answers provided by those that provided answers to the open-ended questions, and those that participated in the focus group discussion so as to determine the veracity of the responses. The analyzed data is presented below in Chapter 4 of this thesis.

CHAPTER FOUR: DATA PRESENTATION, DATA INTERPRETATION, AND DISCUSSION

4.0 Introduction

This Chapter focuses on the presentation of the data collected and analyzed by the researcher; interpretation of the data; and ends with discussion of the findings of the study. The study assessed the impact of the NTBs on Trade Flow within the ECOWAS sub-region, especially between Liberia and Nigeria. The chart below shows the objectives of the study and the research questions of the study.

Chart: Research Objectives and Questions

No.	Objectives of the Research	No.	Research Questions
1.	To Assess the impact of the NTBs on trade flow within the ECOWAS Sub-region, especially between Liberia and Nigeria	1.	How are the NTBs negatively impacting trade within ECOWSS, especially Liberia and Nigeria?
2.	To assess the impact of the NTBs on the traders/ marketers who traveled between Liberia and Nigeria	2.	What are the NTBs that are negatively impacting trade between Liberia and Nigeria?

3.	To identify the NTBs that need to be reformed or eliminated in order for trade to flow between Liberia and Nigeria	3.	What are the NTBs that need to be reformed in order for trade to flow freely between Liberia and Nigeria, and within ECOWAS?
4,	To identify the policies of Liberia and Nigeria that should be reformed in order for trade to flow between the two countries	4.	What national policy reform measures that need to be undertaken in order to improve trade flow between Liberia and Nigeria, and within ECOWAS as a whole?

4.1 Data Presentation

During the study, the researcher tallied the respondents in terms of gender, and nationality of the trader. The researcher also tallied the respondents in terms of the instruments that they responded to, i.e., the open-ended questions, and participation in the focus group discussion. The findings of the study are presented in prose.

Table 3 below presents the respondents by gender (male or female). The Table shows that out of the fifteen (15) respondents that provided answers to the open-ended questions, 3 (20%) were males and 12 (80%) were females. This indicates that more females than males responded to the open- ended questions of the study.

Table 3: - Respondents by Gender

Respondent by Gender	Frequency	Percentage (%)
Male	3	20
Female	12	80
Total	15	100

Source: Researcher's field data, 2020

Table 4 below shows that, of the fifteen respondents that, participated in the focus group discussion, 2 (13%) males participated, while 13 (87%) females participated. Again, the females dominated in the focus group discussion. The questions were the same. The difference was that the open-ended interview questions were administered in person, one-on-one interviews; whereas for the focus group discussion, the discussion was done together. The respondents had the opportunity to correct an answer or buttress an answer.

Table 4: - Focus Group Respondents

Respondent by Gender	Frequency	Percentage (%)
Male	2	13
Female	13	87
Total	15	100

Source: Researcher's field data, 2020

Table 5 below presents respondents by nationality. The Table shows that out of the 30 respondents that participated in the study, 87% (26) were Liberians, while 13% (4) were Nigerians.

Table 5: - Respondents by Nationality

Respondent by national-ity	Frequency	Percentage (%)
Liberians	26	87
Nigerians	4	13
Total	30	100

Source: Researcher's field data, 2020

And finally, Table 6 below presents a consolidation of all the respondents relative to the two instruments used. The table shows that 15 (50%) of the respondents took part in the open ended, one-on-one questions interview, while the balance 15 (50%) took part in the focus group discussion.

Table 6: - Consolidated Respondents by Instruments

Respondents by instruments	Frequency	Percentage (%)
Focus group Group Discussion	15	50
Open ended Questions Respondents	15	50
Total	30	100

Source: Researcher's field data, 2020

The small Liberian business people are making effort to tap on the trade potential within the sub-region, especially Nigeria. The business people travel by road, but sometimes by air. Traveling to Nigeria is easier than returning to Liberia, especially when returning with goods. Traveling from Liberia, the traders take one day to reach Danane, the Liberia-Cote d'Ivoire border, one day to travel to Abidjan; one day to travel from Abidjan to Accra and then to Togo. It takes about three days from Monrovia to Togo; one day from Togo to Nigeria (Lagos), and spend 3-4 days in Nigeria buying goods.

While returning, the traders spend one day from Nigeria to Togo; goods are put on the truck bound for Togo; from Togo to Cote d'Ivoire border with Ghana takes one day, then continue to Abidjan another day. From Abidjan to Danane one day; sleep-over in Danane, and then travel to Loguato checkpoint the next morning, spend the whole day processing customs, sleeps over, and then continue to Monrovia the next day. The traders while traveling to Nigeria without goods face not much difficulties on the road; but when traveling with goods that's when the problem arises.

The traders traveled to Nigeria to import African dresses, lappers, sewed clothes for men and women (men shirts and women blouses); women hair, women shoes, slippers, European dresses, beautification products and cosmetics, spray, etc., according to the respondents.

In order to assess the impact of the NTBs on the traders doing business between Liberia and Nigeria, and ECOWAS, the researcher sought to find answers to the following questions from the respondents (the traders): "(1) What type of goods do you usually buy from Nigeria (or countries in between) and what do you (the trader) carry for sale to Nigeria? (2) How do you travel to and from Nigeria, and how long does it take? (3) How are custom customs procedures affecting the free flow of trade between Liberia and Nigeria? (4) What are your experiences in route (or anywhere in between) to Nigeria and back to Monrovia on business trips? (5) What is your experience regarding payments of extra-money besides the tariff or custom duty for your goods, imports or exports? (6) At what border post do you experience the most difficult and longest inspection procedures? (7) Why do you think this border post is more difficult? (8) What do you think the inspectors look for when you are going to and from Nigeria? (9) What are other experiences that you have had but we did not cover in this interview? And (10) What reform measures would you recommend in order to boost trade between Liberia and Nigeria?

4.2 Data Interpretation

During the study, there were four (4) leading questions in keeping with the objective of the study and the research questions. First, on the question: "What are the NTBs that are negatively affecting the traders/ marketers who traveled between Liberia and Nigeria?", the respondents identified the NTBs as follows: the long delays at custom posts clearing the goods; the emergence of middlemen at customs posts to clear goods; the extortion of money from the traders at checkpoints on the highway; the payment of money for stamping of the ECOWAS Passport (the Book); the levying of tariffs for goods in transit on mere suspicion that the goods will be sold while in transit; the payment of money at check points in order to "drop the gate"; and the non-acceptance of Nigerians traveling with the ECOWAS Passport.

Second, on the question: "How are the NTBs negatively impacting the flow of trade between Nigeria and Liberia?" The respondents' answers were as follows:

1. Long delays at customs posts: there are long customs procedures at the Loguato Customs Border check points, Noway Checkpoint, and the Ghana-Togo border checkpoints. And at every checkpoint, in addition to the tariff, traders are charged extra-money for stamping their passports and/or other unknown reasons. At the Loguato Customs border post, goods are dumped on the ground and counted one-by-one, causing the whole day of delay and sleeping over at the customs post while traveling to Liberia with the goods. If the goods are on the trucks, and the trucks are many, the customs process may take two to three weeks according to the respondents. At the Loguato post, once the goods are opened, they would not be able to recompress the bags, and therefore the transportation cost from Loguato to Monrovia will increase. Also, at the Noway Cote d'Ivoire Border post with Ghana, goods are dumped on the ground and counted one-by-one; and tariffs are levied for every new goods found in the bag, including personal effects. The Loguato and the Noway border posts are said to be the most difficult border posts in route from Liberia to Nigeria, according to the respondents. At the Loguato entry post, in addition to the tariff payment at the customs post, traders are asked to pay 10% and 4% for their goods by the internal revenue collectors (Liberia Revenue Authority).

2. The traders are very much afraid of customs so much so that, if traveling by road, they would prefer to put their goods on the trucks and let the drivers handle the customs procedures and payment of tariff on the highway than bringing the goods by themselves. According to some of the respondents, "money business is too hard on the road". Women officers are used to charge women traders. A respondent said that a "woman officer charged her all over her body until she had to go into the bathroom to come up with the money". Customs duty is treated as a matter between the trader and the customs officer The duty is not revealed

to the trader. There is no known stipulated tariff. The tariff charges can change at any time. In order to avoid this problem, the traders use a middleman or third party to process his/her goods through customs. The traders do not know the tariff for each product being imported.

3. There are just too many checkpoints on the highway, where bribery and corruption are high. At every checkpoint, the traders are asked to pay money in order for the security officers to "put the gate down". Sometimes the charge is 1000 CFA, 2000CFA, 5000CFA in Cote D'Ivoire. There is no fixed charge for putting the gate down. All these extra-money payments add up to the cost of the business, and many small business people have lost business and stopped going to Nigeria to do business. The respondents said they were operating at a loss. There are also five checkpoints from the Ghana border with Cote d'Ivoire to Ghana-Togo border. And at all those checkpoints, traders must pay money, sometime 5 Cedes, 10 Cedes, 20 Cedes, etc. There is no fixed charge; traders must be prepared for it.

4. The traders, though citizens of ECOWAS member states, are not allowed to travel freely within ECOWAS countries even with ECOWAS Passport. Respondents said that once the security officers see a trader with the ECOWAS passport, he/she is asked to pay extra money for stamping of the Book. While others are paying 1000CFA, those with ECOWAS Passport will be asked to pay 2,500 CFA/ or 5000 CFA. This is a sign of non-recognition of the ECOWAS Passport. The stamping of ECOWAS Passport (the Book) is done at every border entry point, and money must be paid for stamping. In order to stamp the Book, or the Passport in Ghana, the charge is the equivalent of 1,000 CFA: while in Cote d'Ivoire the charge is 2,000 CFA, and for Togo, it is 3,000 CFA. The ECOWAS Passport is a fulfillment of ECOWAS Protocol that allows for free movement of people within the 16 member states of ECOWAS.

5. The Nigerians feel rejected in West Africa. The respondents claimed that because they carried Nigerian Passport, they are

charged higher amounts at border entry points. For example, while other nationals are paying 2,000 CFA to have their book or passport stamp, Nigerians are charged 10,000 CFA. The respondent said that as Nigerians, they are perceived as "criminals and drugs smugglers". On the highway, when a Nigerian does not pay the money, he/she is not allowed to continue on the journey. A respondent had similar experience at the Clay Junction / Iron gate in Bomi County while in route to Monrovia, Liberia.

Even in Liberia, Nigerians do not feel accepted. They are seen as criminals and drug dealers. One of the respondents had a personal encounter with a Drug Enforcement Agency (DEA) officer in Monrovia. A DEA officer held the Nigerian on suspicion that the Nigerian was carrying drugs on his body. The Nigerian was traveling from Clara Town where he lives to Waterside where he does his business. He was held by the DEA Officer at their office from 8 a.m. to 5 p.m., but did not find any drug on him rather the DEA Officer took US$10.00, some naira and L$300.00 that he (Nigerian) had in his pocket. According to the respondent, Liberians insult Nigerians doing business in Liberia. The respondents claimed that they (Nigerians) bring money to Liberia to do business, and it is their ability and entrepreneurship that make the money to grow.

At checkpoints, Nigerians are treated with suspicion, "once you present a Nigerian Passport". The custom officers believe that Nigerians have money, therefore, they (customs officers) must get their share. While traveling by road, the traders pay a lot of money, according to the respondents. There is a lot of exploitation at the borders. Cote d'Ivoire is the most difficult route to travel for business; Mali and Ghana are the easier routes to travel, according to the respondents. After crossing the borders, there are yet a lot of payment demands at checkpoints in Cote d'Ivoire. For this reason, traders take the bus to travel to Cote d' Ivoire from Accra. At the border posts, the custom officers dump the bags of the traders while looking for Jewry, tablets, drugs and undeclared goods. As long as a trader presents a Nigerian Passport, he/she is search for drug, according to the respondents

6. The presence of middlemen: Traders are very much afraid of the customs officers and customs procedures. Therefore, the traders give their goods to the middlemen who process them through custom/checkpoints. The traders pay the middlemen for their services, which adds up to the cost of the business. The actual tariff for the goods is not revealed to the traders nor displayed at the customs posts, so the traders do not know how much extra the middlemen are taking for their services.

7. The existence of the truck cartels: Because of fear of customs procedures, the traders put their goods on the trucks bound for Monrovia. The trader is charged US$100.00, US$150,00, US$250.00, etc., per bag from Togo to Monrovia, depending on the quantity of the goods in the bag. The goods are delivered to the trader in Monrovia after payment is made. The truck drivers do not give receipts to the traders for the tariff or other services performed on their (traders) behalf at the various customs posts and checkpoints while transporting the goods.

The truck drivers decide on how much to charge and how much to pay in route to Monrovia. Traders have not much to negotiate for in the process. Sometimes the goods will reach Monrovia within two-three weeks on the truck traveling from Togo to Monrovia. But if there is closure of borders by one country or another in route, the goods will further delay and the trader would be at a loss, especially when the goods are purchased in order to be sold during the festive season, like Liberia's Independence Day, July 26 or Christmas Day, December 25.

(8. The most difficult travel route: Most of the respondents said the most difficult travel route is the Cote d'Ivoire Highway, from Danane on the border with Liberia to Abidjan, then to "Noway" Border check point with Ghana. The security officers are hash and uncompromising. When they ask for money and is not paid, the trader wouldn't be allowed to continue on the journey.

9. Old office equipment and facilities at the Liberia's Loguato Customs Post: The Loguato post does not have computers; therefore, they use typewriters, which leads to delay in the customs clearing process. Some traders consider the Loguato custom post to be the most difficult and time-consuming post on that highway.

(10) Payment of customs duty for goods in transit: The respondents said that they have to pay customs duty at every port of entry because of suspicion that the goods may be sold while in transit.

Third, on the question: "What are the NTBs that need to be reformed in order for trade to flow freely between Liberia and Nigeria, and within ECOWAS, the respondents said that all the NTBs identified need to be reformed or eliminated. The long delays at the customs posts need to be curtailed by improving the services at the customs posts. This can be done by deploying modern facilities such as computers and other office equipment. But most importantly, a policy decision needs to be taken at the ministerial or presidential levels by the ECOWAS Heads of State and Governments to regulate, in term of time, how long should goods stay at a border post while being processed. Second, the tariff schedule should be displayed at the customs post for all traders to see so that they (traders) wouldn't be overly charged by the middlemen in order to process their goods through customs. The governments of ECOWAS member states, especially Liberia, Cote d'Ivoire, Ghana, Togo, Benin, and Nigeria should remove the internal checkpoints that unnecessarily restrict the movement of traders and their goods. Once the travel documents are valid and tariffs paid for the goods, there should not be any other hindrance while in route to do their business. And third, all ECOWAS member states should recognize the ECOWAS Passport as legitimate travel document, and therefore shouldn't charge the traders for stamping the Book. The member states of ECOWAS should take steps to stop the harassment of traders traveling to do business in the ECOWAS sub-region.

Fourth, on the question: what national policy reform measures that need to be undertaken in order to improve trade flow between Liberia and Nigeria, and within ECOWAS as a whole, the respondents said that at the national levels (Liberia and Nigeria), the governments of the two countries should review their local trade policies and take steps to increasing trade between the two countries. While most of the respondents travel to Nigeria to buy dry goods, such as women's and men's wears, lappers, sewed clothes, etc., they carry nothing to Nigeria to sell. There is a need for Liberia and Nigeria to redirect their respective trade destination within the context of intra-ECOWAS trade, and increase the volume of trade between the two countries. The two countries should hold trade negotiations, identify common areas of trade interest and forge such interest. Nigeria can assist Liberia in upgrading the National Standard Laboratory so that it (the lab) can receive the required certification that will enable Liberian business people to export their plant and animal products in keeping with the WTO Sanitary and Pyto-sanitary Standards. Nigeria and Liberia should endeavor to implement the CET, the ETLS: and for Liberia the WTO Post-Accession Plan so that it can benefit from broader market access in other parts of the world.

4. 3 Discussion of Findings

The key research problem in this study was that irrespective of the fact that Nigeria and Liberia are both members of ECOWAS, the trade flow between the two countries has been very marginal. Liberia has not been able to tap on the vast Nigerian market of over one hundred million consumers. The marginal performance has been attributed partly to the high level of Non-tariff Barriers (NTBs) that continue to exist in ECOWAS member states, especially Liberia, Cote d'Ivoire, Ghana, Togo, Benin, and Nigeria, which are the trade routes and destinations of the traders in this study. Therefore, the study examines the impact of NTBs on trade flow within ECOWAS, especially between Liberia and Nigeria.

The impact of NTBs on the growth of trade and commerce within the sub-region; and on the traders in terms of business and /or opportunity lost.

The research questions therefore were: (1) What are the NTBs that are negatively impacting trade flow between Liberia and Nigeria? (2) How are the NTBs affecting the traders/ marketers who traveled between Liberia and Nigeria? (3) What are the NTBs that need to be reformed in order for trade to flow freely between Liberia and Nigeria, and within ECOWAS? (4) What national policy reform measures that need to be undertaken in order to improve trade flow between Liberia and Nigeria, and within ECOWAS as a whole?

The target population for this research was the traders/ marketers who traveled from Waterside (Monrovia-Liberia) to do business in Nigeria and the countries in between. A simple random sampling technique was used to select the respondents, and open-ended interview questions were administered, and a focus group discussion held with the respondents.

Data analysis and interpretation revealed two major findings: (1) that indeed the NTBs do exist and are affecting trade flow between Liberia and Nigeria. The first objective of this study was to find out the NTBs that are negatively affecting the flow of trade between Liberia and Nigeria. The NTBs identified are (a) long customs procedures at the posts of entry between the six countries (Liberia, Cote D'Ivoire, Ghana, Togo, Benin and Nigeria). (b)The customs officers and other security officers demand payments for goods in transit; (c) the high-level of corruption and bribery on the highway and check points, security officers demanding money from the traders; (d) extorting money for stamping the ECOWAS Passports, which should not be the case; (e) cumbersome customs procedures, leading to the emergence of middlemen, which is another layer of cost for the traders; (f) not revealing of tariff and other trade information (e.g., ETLS) that the traders could take advantage of; and (g) the existence of truck cartels that have a virtual monopoly over the transportation of goods from Nigeria to Liberia. The cartels decide on the transportation fare, the cost for taking the goods from Togo to Liberia via Abidjan. This study confirmed that, indeed, there are NTBs that are negatively affecting trade flows between Liberia and Nigeria. The NTBs make the cost of doing business high not only in terms of money but also the inconveniences and harassment of the traders on the highway.

Krugman and Obsfield, in their book, International Economics, Theory and Policy, Third Edition indicated that countries trade because of two reasons: (1) the countries are different; (2) when countries trade, they achieve economies of scale in production. That is to say, each country will produce a limited range of goods that can be produced at a larger scale and more efficiently than when one country tries to produce all the goods (self-sufficiency) (Krugman and Obsfield, 1994, pp. 3-4). In short, trade provides benefits by allowing to export goods whose production makes relatively heavy use of resources that are locally abundant, while importing goods whose production makes heavy use of resources that are locally scare. Thus, it will lead to mutual gains from trade between the two countries. A country will specialize in the production of goods and services in which it has comparative advantage. The gain from trade can be in two forms: specialization (which increases production possibilities), and consumption possibility (Krugman and Obsfield, 1994, pp. 17-18). In this way, a range of consumption choices will be enlarged and the two countries will be better off.

An absolute production advantage over other countries in producing a good is neither a necessary or sufficient condition for having a comparative advantage in the good. The comparative advantage of an industry depends not only on its productivity relative to the foreign industry, but also on the domestic wage relative to the foreign wage. Therefore, a country's wage rate depends on the relative productivity in its other industries (Krugman and Obsfield, 1994, p. 182). In this connection, Nigeria and Liberia can mutually benefit from trade if they take advantage of trade in order to increase their production and consumption possibilities. Some governments use Non-tariff Barriers to protect their domestic industries (Krugman and Obsfield, 1994, pp. 196, 201). But the NTBs identified under this study are unnecessary. They are not intended to protect local industries, but they are a source of inefficiencies and hindrance to trade facilitation. Within the context of trade liberalization, if the NTBs remain in place, reduction in tariff will have no upward effect on trade flow.

(2) Relative to the second key question as to "how the NTBs are negatively affecting the traders/ marketers who traveled between Liberia and Nigeria", the study finds out that traders faced untold hardship on their way from Nigeria for the purpose of doing business. They faced harassment in the hands of security officers at check points, customs and border posts, demanding money and/or taking some of their items away unnecessarily. All this adds up to the high cost of doing business within the ECOWAS sub-region, which drives some small traders out of business.

Harris et al (2011), define NTBs as anything other than tariff that restricts trade. They argue that the high prevalence of NTBs is in part driven by the pace of liberalization and integration; that the fear of inadequate protection for local producers has facilitated the proliferation of NTBs in the region. The integration in West Africa is a pile of rules and pact work, with no genuine scope of implementation (Engel and Jouanjean, 2013).

The main feature of the ECOWAS' trade policy is the ECOWAS Trade Liberalization Scheme, which was adopted in 1979. The objective of the Scheme is to progressively establish a customs union among the member states of ECOWAS. The customs union will, inter alia, evolve the elimination of customs duties and taxes of equivalent effect. The ECOWAS Trade Liberalization Scheme covers three groups of products, i.e., unprocessed goods, traditional handicraft products, and industrial products (Essien 2006, pp2-3) (Fajana, 2018 p.vi), but the ETLS has not been fully implemented by ECOWAS member states.

Accordingly, there is a need for ECOWAS member states to be more firm about the establishment of the ECOWAS free trade area, and implement progressively the ETLS and the CET if intra-ECOWAS trade is to boom between and amongst the countries of West Africa. Under the ETLS, products produced locally can be traded within ECOWAS sub-region free of customs duties and levies in keeping with ECOWAS protocols. And Liberia's strategy is gradual implementation of ECOWAS protocols, according to its national trade policy.

The ECOWAS sub-region has the largest number of legal agreements, including the ECOWAS Protocol on the Free Movement of Persons and Goods (1978) and the ECOWAS Trade Liberalization Scheme (ETLS - 1979), the main operational tool for promoting West Africa as a free trade area. The ECOWAS' trade policy was designed to increase intra-regional commerce, raise trade volume and generally galvanize the economic activities within the region in such a way as to positively impact on the economic wellbeing of ECOWAS citizens (Essien 2006, p 2).

The ECOWAS' trade policy is also meant to foster smooth integration of the sub-region into the world economy, with due regard for the political choices and development priorities of states in their desire to engender sustainable development and reduction of poverty. The ECOWAS' CET which was launched in 2015 stipulates that there will exist within ECOWAS member states a uniform tariff for all goods imported from non-ECOWAS member countries. The CET is an important milestone in the creation of a customs union for West Africa (https://www.ecowas. int/ecowas-sectors/trade/).

However, the NTBs restrict the flow of trade (Harris, Chambers & Foresti, 2011). Most ECOWAS member states, for example Liberia (MoCI Annual Report, 2017) are reluctant to raise their tariff from 5.3% to 13% in order to meet the CET tariff level. Implementation of the ETLS would ensure that locally produced goods are traded free of tariffs in the ECOWAS member states (MoCI Annual Report, 2017)

Nigeria, the largest market in West Africa, has little intra-ECOWAS trade compared to Asia, Europe and the Americas

(Oluwasola and Adesanya, 2012). Nigeria's trade policy has been inward looking, short-term and restrictive in nature, and directed at meeting specific objectives, such as, ensuring balance of payments viability and promotion. They were also meant to complement other policy initiatives, such as industrialization policy, employment creation and self-sufficiency policies, etc. (Analogbei, 2012). Irrespective of the fact that Nigeria has a comparative advantage in almost all traded goods in West Africa, Nigeria and the rest of the West African countries can be better off (gain from trade) if they increase their trade levels between and among themselves (Krugman and Obsfield, 1994, p. 17-18), creating a free trade area in line with the objectives of ECOWAS.

On the other hand, Liberia has been pursuing in recent time a liberal trade policy, starting with the open-door policy to the Liberia national trade policy of 2014. Its current trade policy is centered around export competitiveness, strengthening domestic trade and local productive capacity, and the promotion of regional and international trade (LNTP, 2014). Liberia is a founding member of ECOWAS, a customs union, and its goal is to increase participation and gain from the vast ECOWAS market of 16 countries. However, the problem with Liberia is that it is beset by structural bottleneck, in terms of lack of technical infrastructure for trade facilitation, and the quality of standards to meeting international requirements. Liberia's exports are limited to few primary commodities and few destination markets. Liberia's capacity for effective participation in the global market is limited, and the quality of goods and services produced are of low quality (LNTP, 2014). The small Liberian business people do not take goods with them to Nigeria to sell. They go and buy in order to sell on the Liberian market. Also, Liberia has not taken policy and administrative measures to eliminate the high-level of NTBs at the Loguato border post that continue to restrict the free flow of goods from Nigeria to Liberia. The wide spread corruption at check points on the highway is a tacit endorsement by the governments of West Africa because they are doing nothing to stop it. The governments must agree at the highest level to eradicate the NTBs, if trade is to flow freely and expand in West Africa, particularly between Liberia and Nigeria. The implementation of the ETLS will ensure that locally produced goods are traded free of tariff in ECOWAS member states

The Liberia National Trade Policy supports trade facilitation, improvement in trade and transit infrastructure for smooth flow of goods and services across its border. Therefore, trade facilitation is an essential component of Liberia's trade policy. Liberia's trade policy recognizes the need to remove non-tariff barrier measures in order to achieve regional integration, the implementation of the ETLS and the CET (LNTP, 2014). However, in order to support regional integration, the LNTP addresses the implementation of the ECOWAS Trade Liberalization Scheme and Common External Tariff, the progressive reduction of regional non-tariff measures and trade-related bottlenecks, and the promotion of wider African trade integration.

CHAPTER FIVE: SUMMARY, CONCLUSION AND RECOMMENDATIONS

5.0 Introduction

This Chapter covers three main sections, i.e., Summary of the findings, the Conclusion, and Operational and Policy Recommendations.

5.1 Summary of key findings

The main NTBs affecting trade between Liberia and Nigeria are the long custom procedures; the too many check points on the highway between Liberia and Nigeria, and all the countries in between (Cote d'Ivoire, Ghana, Togo, Benin); the extortion of extra-money beyond the tariff for the goods. The too many checkpoints are the main source of bribery and corruption on the highways. The cumbersome customs procedures caused the emergence of middlemen just to clear the goods through customs. There is constant harassment of traders for money on the highway, in the name of "dropping the gate", and/or looking for illicit drugs, undeclared or under declared goods. The traders also paid for goods in transit, which is against the ECOWAS trade protocols.

Almost all the ECOWAS member states are not fully implementing the protocols of ECOWAS in terms of the ETLS and the CET. The NTBs are negatively affecting the flow of trade between Liberia and Nigeria. Consequently, the goods flow to Liberia is difficult. The study also shows that the trade between Liberia and Nigeria is "one-way". Liberians travel to Nigeria to buy goods to sell in the Liberian market, but do not carry goods to Nigeria to sell. Liberian traders don't have the capacity to export to Nigeria, and also most Liberian products do not meet international standards for export, especially animal and plant products. The Liberian trade policy is good, but implementation is faced with technical constraints. On the other hand, Nigeria's trade policy is more outward looking in terms of directing its trade to Europe, Asia and the Americas, as compared to intra-ECOWAS trade.

Nonetheless, international economic trade theories have shown that, irrespective of the country comparative advantage in the production of all goods and services, it could still trade with a country (ies) with less comparative advantage, taking into consideration the endowment of the factors of production and price relativity. So, Nigeria can increase its trade within West Africa and still meet its trade policy objectives and balance of payment concerns.

5.2 Conclusion

Indeed, there is clear evidence that the NTBs are many and are negatively affecting the flow of trade between Liberia and Nigeria. The long and tedious custom procedures, the harassment of traders for money on the highway, the high cost of using the trucks to carry goods to Monrovia are impacting negatively on the flow of trade between Nigeria and Liberia. In order to improve trade flow between the two countries, policy reforms must be taken at the inter-governmental summit level or at ECOWAS in order to remove the NTBs. Liberia and Nigeria and other ECOWAS member states should make concerted effort at improving trade flow within the sub-region.

The too many check points should be removed from the highway and the ETLS and the CET should be implemented in order to increase the volume of trade between and amongst ECOWAS member states. There is clear evidence that member states of ECOWAS are not taking steps to stop the high-level of corruption and bribery on the highway, and at customs border posts between Liberia and Nigeria (and all the countries in between) by customs and security officers. This represents a tacit approval by the governments of the respective countries and by ECOWAS for such unwholesome practices to continue. This runs contrary to the policy objectives of ECOWAS' ETLS on free movement of goods and people.

Also, irrespective of the fact that Nigeria has a comparative advantage in the production of almost all goods and services, there is still room for trade to flourish between the two countries, especially within the context of intra-ECOWAS trade bloc. ECOWAS should set up its trade facilitation drive, and insist on the creation of the customs union, a free trade area of the 16 countries, and the implementation of the ETLS and CET.

5.3 Recommendations

Having gone through this study and obtained valuable findings from the responses of the respondents, this researcher proposes the following recommendations relative to the treatment of the NTBs and the improvement of trade flow between Liberia and Nigeria, and within West Africa.

5.3.1 Operational recommendations

1. The Governments of Liberia, Cote d'Ivoire, Ghana, Togo, Benin and Nigeria should improve services at their respectively customs border posts. The customs procedures are long and cumbersome. This can be done by replacing the old office equipment such as typewriters with computers

and other modern office facilities so as to speed up the customs processes.

2.   The Liberian Government should put in place a scanner at the Liberia's Loguato Customs Border Post so as to prevent the tearing of bags in order to see the content therein. The current customs procedure is an NTB because it causes long delays and inconveniences for the traders.

3.   Curtail the payment of "extra money" to customs, immigration, police and other security officers at the customs border posts and on the highway just to "drop the gates", etc. This has become notorious and is affecting trade flow between Liberia and Nigeria, and the countries in route to Nigeria, i.e., Cote d'Ivoire, Ghana, Togo and Benin.

4.   The governments of the ECOWAS member countries, especially Liberia, Cote D'Ivoire, Ghana, Togo, Benin and Nigeria should remove the too many checkpoints on the highway. These checkpoints are the main source of corruption and bribery facing traders doing business between Liberia and Nigeria. The removal of checkpoints will eliminate or minimize the extortion of money from traders while in route to do business.

5.   The government of Liberia should provide better social facilities at the Loguato Customs Boarder Post, including bathroom and toilet facilities for traders passing through the customs post. The government should also provide low-cost housing facilities for the traders sleeping overnight to clear their goods.

5.3.2 Policy recommendations

1. Curtail payment of custom duties or charges for goods in transit from the country of purchase to the country of sale. This is against normal trade practice. Custom duties are levied on goods at the country where final sale is to be made, but not in transit. There are too many payments even for goods in transit from Togo

to Ghana, then to Cote d'Ivoire, then to Liberia customs post. Customs officers levy customs duties on every item, including personal effects (carryover bags), once the items are new.

2. Requesting payments for stamping of the ECOWAS Passport should be stopped. The money does not go into the coffers of the governments but into the pockets of the security officers.

3. The governments of Liberia and Nigeria, and countries in between, or ECOWAS should make it a policy that the tariff schedule for goods should be displayed at the various custom posts and other places, including social media, radio, customs' bulletin boards, etc. so that the traders can be informed of the tariff to pay for the goods being imported. The traders trade at the "will and pleasure" of the middlemen who decides on how much a trader should pay for the goods being imported. The traders do not know the tariff, and therefore, cannot negotiate effectively.

4. ECOWAS member states should treat all citizens/ traders equally. ECOWAS member states should recognize and accept the ECOWAS Passport as a legitimate travel document at all posts of entry in Liberia, Cote d'Ivoire, Ghana, Togo, Benin and Nigeria, as well as other ECOWAS member states. Customs officers of ECOWAS member states should not charge for stamping the ECOWAS Passport (the Book). The demand for money is too much while traveling for business with ECOWAS Passports, according to the respondents. Traders should be allowed to travel freely as long as their travel documents are valid. In Cote d'Ivoire, Liberians are asked to pay extra money when traveling with ECOWAS Passports.

5. The customs officers at the various posts of entry should stop the use of agents or middlemen to process customs duties, especially at the Loguato, Noway and the Ghana-Togo border posts. The middlemen charged the traders too much money in order to process their goods through customs. The respondents said that if they are brave to do the customs process themselves, they won't know what to expect because the tariff is not revealed to them. If the tariff is revealed, the traders will be able to negotiate with the middlemen for their services.

6. All ECOWAS citizens should be treated equally and accepted by everyone. Nigerians should be accepted by other West Africans. Nigerians shouldn't be treated as drug dealers or traveling with drug money. If Nigerians succeed in business in Liberia, they will invite Liberians into partnership. Nigerians should be given space to do business in Liberia. Nigerians shouldn't be harassed by Liberian security as well as other people. Nigerians should be treated the same as other traders. Nigerians shouldn't be compelled to pay 10,000LD, while others are paying 5,000LD for the same service.

7. Increase competition among truck drivers doing business between Liberia and Nigeria. In this way, the truck cartel will cease to exist. The more trucks on the route to do business, the less the power of the cartel to operate as a monopoly, controlling the entire transport value chain, setting their own transport fare and controlling customs services for the traders; thus, exploiting the traders and increasing the cost of doing business within the ECOWAS region, especially between Liberia and Nigeria. In this way, more traders will go for business to Nigeria and the countries in between, and more trucks will follow the business. With competition amongst the truck drivers, the transport cost for traders will reduced, and traders will do more business; and the business flow between Liberia and Nigeria will increase. Traders want to travel with their goods but because of the so much harassment at checkpoints, they are compelled to allow the truck drivers to handle the transportation and customs process for their goods (thus falling from the frying pan (security officers) into the fire (truck drivers), the cost of doing business continue to increase). Traders suffered higher cost and delay in the transportation of their goods from Nigeria to Togo then to Monrovia, Liberia.

8. The governments of the two countries (Liberia and Nigeria) should review their local trade policies and take steps to increasing trade between the two countries. While most of the respondents travel to Nigeria to buy dry goods, such as women and men wears, lappers, sewed clothes, etc. they carry nothing to Nigeria to sell. There is a need for Liberia and Nigeria to redirect their respective

trade destinations, within the context of intra-ECOWAS trade and increase the volume of trade between the two countries. The two countries should hold trade negotiations, identify common areas of trade interest and forge such interest. Nigeria can assist Liberia in upgrading the National Standard Laboratory so that it (the lab) can receive the required certification that will enable Liberian business people to export their plant and animal products in keeping with the WTO Sanitary and Pyto-sanitary Standards. Nigeria and Liberia should endeavor to implement the CET, the ETLS: and for Liberia, the WTO post accession plan so that it can benefit from increased market access in other parts of the world.

REFERENCES

African Continental Free Trade Area (AfCFTA) Legal Texts and Policy Documents
(https://www.tralac.org/resources/by-region/cfta.html#ratification)

Analogbei, F. C. O. (1912). Trade Reform and Productivity in Nigeria.

Anonymous- Knowing the Third World: Colonial Encounter (anonymous)

Anonymous - Knowing the Third World, Development Decades

Bhat, Adi. (2009). Research Design: Definition, Characteristics and Types. Introduction
to Qualitative Research, 4th Edition, SAGE.

Deeb, T. and Humado, K. (2007) "SPS Synthesis Report" WATH/Accra Technical
Report No. 20.

ECOWAS (2008), "ECOWAP at a Glance" ECOWAS Commission
https://www.ecowas.int/ecowas-sectors/trade/

Engel, Jakob and Jouanjean, Marie-Agnes. (2013). Barrier to Trade in Food Staples in West Africa: An Analytical Review. ODI

Epiphane G. ADJOVI and Dr Alioune NIANG, (2015). the Potential Gains of a Continental

Free Trade Area for the Economic and Social Condition of ECOWAS Citizens,
Briefing papers

http://endacacid.org/latest/index.php?option=com_
content&view=article&id=1016:the-potentiel-gains-of-a-
continental-free-trade-area-for-the-economic-and-social-
conditions-of-eecowas-citizens&catid=275:mp-pgr-cgef-
actualites&Itemid=1563

Essien, Victor, (2006) Regional Trade Agreements in Africa:
A Historical and Bibliographic

Account of ECOWAS and CEMAC, Fordham Law School.
https://www.nyulawglobal.org/globalex/CEMAC_
ECOWAS.html

Fajana, Olufell (2018), Accelerating the implementation of
the ECOWAS Trade

Liberation Scheme, UNECA.

Fangiun, Cao, (2009) Modern Theory and China's Road to
Modernization; Chinese Studies

in History; Vol. 43. Nol.

FOWDAD, Regionalism and the Global Economy, the case
of Africa, 1996

Fred P.M. van der Kraaij, (1983) 'The Open-Door Policy of
Liberia. An Economic

History of Modern Liberia' (Bremen, 1983), Chapter 2, The
origins of the Closed-Door Policies and Open-Door Policies 1847-
1947, pp. 12-46.

GOL, Liberia National Trade Policy, 2014 – 2019

GOL, Ministry of Commerce and Industry, Annual Report,
2016

GOL, Ministry of Commerce and Industry, Annual Report
2017

Harris, D., V. Chambers and M. Foresti (2011) "The Political
Economy of Regional

Integration and Regionalism in West Africa: A
Scoping Exercise"

https://www.ecowas.int/ecowas-sectors/trade/   ECOWAS
2016

Irogbe, Kima, (2005). Globalization and the Development of Underdevelopment of the

Third World, Claflin University, Orengeburg, South Carolina Journal of their world studies, Vol. XXII no. 1.

Kalu, Ude Damian and Agodi Joy E. (2015) Does Trade Openness Make Sense? Investigation

of Nigeria Trade Policy. International Journal of Academic Research and Social Sciences, 2015, Vol.4 No. 1

Keane, Jodie, Massimiliano Cali & Jane Kennan (2010) Impediments to Intra- Regional Trade in Sub-Saharan Africa, Overseas Development Institute.

Kraaij, Fred P.M.van der (1983), the Open-Door Policy of Liberia: An Economic History of Modern Liberia (Bremen, 1983) Chapter 2 the Origins of the Closed-Door Policies and the Open-door Policies, 1847 – 1947, pp. 12 - 46

Krugman, Paul and Maurice Obsfield, (1994). International Economics, Theory and Policy,

3rd Edition, HarperCollinsCollegePublisher, USA

Lavrakas, P.J., (2008) Encyclopedia of Survey Research Methods (vol 1-0)) SAGE

Publications.

Melo, James de, and Mancellari, Armela (2013). Regional And Global Trade Strategies for

Liberia (working Paper) International Growth Center, Dec. 2013 Mwasha, Ombeni N. (2002). The Benefits of Regional Economic Integration for Developing Countries in Africa: A Case of East African Community (EAC), 2007 EAC official website (www.eac.int), EAC Development Strategy 2006-2010 and the treaty for the establishment of EAC.

Omoju, Oluwasola & Olumide Adesanya, (2012). Does Trade Promote Growth in Developing Countries? Empirical Evidence from Nigeria, International Journal of Development and Sustainability Online ISSN: 2168-8662 – www.isdsnet. com/ijds Volume 1 Number 3: Pages 743-753 ISDS Article ID: IJDS12092701. National Institute for Legislative Studies,

Abuja, Nigeria Research Instruments Examples, Teachers College, Columbia University, N.Y., N.Y, 10027

Rodrik, Dani, (1998) Trade Policy and Economic Performance in Sub-Saharan Africa,

Working paper series 6562; NBER (National Bureau of Economic Research), John F. Kennedy, School of Government, Harvard University, 79 J.F.K Street, Cambridge, MA 02138

Shukla, S. P., (2000). From GATT to WTO and Beyond, Working Papers No. 195.

The United Nations University WIDER (World Institute for Development Economic Research), 2000

Stebbins, Robert A. (2011). Exploratory Research in Social Science,

SAGE Research Methods, 2011

Tamuno, Steve Otonye, and Edoumiekumo, 2012, Industrialization and Trade Globalization:

What Hope for Nigeria. International Journal of Academic Research and Social Sciences, June 2012 Vol.2 No. 6

The WTO and GATT: A Principled History

https://www.brookings.edu/wpcontent/uploads/2016/07/selfenforcingtrade_chapter.pdf

APPENDIX A – LETTER OF PERMISSION TO CONDUCT RESEARCH

University of Liberia

July 13, 2020

<u>TO WHOM IT MAY CONCERN</u>

We present compliments and wish to introduce and recommend to you student **Ramses T. Kumbuyah** of the Ibrahim Badamasi Babangida Graduate School of International Studies, University of Liberia, who is writing his Graduate Thesis.

Student Ramses T. Kumbuyah is undertaking thesis topic: **"An Assessment of the Impact of Non-Tariff Barriers on the Flow of International Trade within the ECOWAS Sub-Region: A case study of Trade Flows Between the Republic of Liberia and Nigeria (2015 -2019)"**, and will need your assistance to successfully complete the study.

In view of the above, we are kindly requesting your assistance to enable student Ramses T. Kumbuyah conduct his research in the study area, as we assure you that the result of the research will only be used for academic purpose.

Thanks for your kind consideration in the premises.

Sincerely yours,

Van K. Clinton
Administrative Assistant to the Director
Cell#: 0776001000/0886538856
Email: <u>vclinton18@gmail.com</u>

APPENDIX B - INFORMED CONSENT FORM

Research Topic: Assessment of the Impact of Non-Tariff Barriers on the Flow of International

Trade within the ECOWAS Sub-Region: A Case Study of Trade Flows Between the Republics of Liberia and Nigeria (2015 – 2019)

Name of Researcher: Ramses Tamba Kumbuyah, Masters Candidate, University of Liberia Graduate School of International Studies:**Summary of the Study:** The study will investigate how the Non-Tariff Barriers (NTBs) are impacting the flow of trade within ECOWAS, and most especially between Liberia and Nigeria. How the NTBs are affecting the traders that travelled from Monrovia through Cote D'Ivoire, Ghana, Togo, Benin then to Nigeria and back to Monrovia. The Non-Tariff Barriers are defined as anything, i.e., the non-trade measures, other than tariffs or custom duties, that restrict trade. The study will examine other non-trade measures that the traders are faced with as they travel on that road to do business. The study will also examine policies of Liberia, Nigeria, ECOWAS and WTO and how they affect trade and industrial growth in the sub-region. All other things held constant, the interview will last for thirty minutes per interviewer to complete the open-ended questions; and about forty-five minutes to complete the focused group interview.

1. I confirm that I have read and understand the summary for the above study and have had the opportunity to ask questions.
2. I understand that my participation is voluntary and that I am free to withdraw at any time, without giving any reason.
3. I understand that by participating in this study I will not be referred to or identified by name in any publications arising from this study.

4. I agree to take part in the above study voluntarily

____

Name of Participant   Date   Participant's Signature

_________________   __________   ________________

Researcher   Date   Signature

UNIVERSITY OF LIBERIA

Ibrahim Badamasi Babangida Graduate School of Interntional Studies Final Thesis Research Instrument

Research Topic: Assessment of the Impact of Non-Tariff Barriers on the Flow of International Trade within the ECOWAS Sub-Region: A Case Study of Trade Flow Between the Republics of Liberia and Nigeria (2015 – 2019)

1. What type of goods do you normally buy from Nigeria (or counties in between) and what do you carry for sale to Nigeria?
2. How do you travel to and from Nigeria, and how long does it take?
3. How are customs procedures affecting the free flow of trade between Liberia and Nigeria"?
4. What are your experiences in route (or anywhere in between) to Nigeria and back to Liberia to do business, in terms of check points and points of entry?
5. What is your experience regarding the payment of extra-money besides the tariff or custom duty for your goods, imports or exports?
6. At what border post do you experience the most difficult and longest inspection procedures?
7. Why do you think this border post is the most difficult one?
8. What is it that the inspectors look for when you are going to and coming from Nigeria?
9. What are other experiences that you have had but we did not cover in this interview?
10. What reform measures would you recommend in order to boost trade between Liberia and Nigeria?

APPENDIX D - NON – TRADE BARRIERS IN WEST AFRICA

Case Study of the Impact of Non-tariff Barriers on Trade Flow between Liberia and Nigeria (2015 - 2019)

Non-tariff Trade Barriers In West Africa (Harris, Chambers &Foresti (2011) Country	Non-Implementation of ECOWAS Trade Liberalization Scheme (ETLS)
Burkina Faso	**Application of non-tariff barriers at borders and on transport routes:** In addition to seasonal restrictions listed separately below, illegal road stops and demands for bribes constituted common non-tariff barriers persisting along main transport corridors. Refusal to pay the money demanded could result in significant delays.
Burkina Faso	**Improper Charging of Duty to Value-added Goods:** Despite ETLS provisions that goods with 30% value added are to enter duty free provided they are accompanied by a certificate of origin, half of the private sector respondents reported being required to pay duty on such products. Such practices reduce incentives for value addition in the region and increase costs for manufacturers and processors. Higher costs reduce the competitiveness of West African products in both external and intra-regional markets.

Burkina Faso	**Application of Seasonal Restrictions:** The application by Burkina Faso of seasonal restrictions on certain products, most notably maize, has mwultiple negative impacts, including the reduction of farmers' income. The seasonal restrictions imposed also compromise regional food availability and security during the off-season. Respondents highlighted the fact that by paying bribes, exports are still possible in spite of these restrictions.
Burkina Faso	**Limits on truck axle loads are not being followed:** ECOWAS protocols limit axle loads to 11.5 tonnes per axle. Inconsistent application of this limit increases transport costs, exacerbates and accelerates road destruction, causes more frequent accidents when trucks are structurally unsound, and encourages unoficial payments.
Benin	**Gap between Legislation and Implementation:** The Gap Analysis research team was unable to find updated legislation, regulation or procedures addressing many of the ETLS protocols. As in many countries, there is a lack of enforcement and consistency in application of national or regional laws at the borders. In addition, unoficial non-tariff barriers (NTBs) are also sometimes imposed at borders.
Benin	**Low Private-Sector Awareness of ETLS:** Private-sector traders indicated they had limited, detailed information on ETLS protocols, their rights, where to find information and documents needed for transit across borders, and the normal fees for processing.

Benin	**Inter-State Road Transit (ISRT) Guarantee Bond and Logbook are not functioning:** Use of a uniform customs transit, declaration and bond system such as the ISRT is necessary for facilitating regional trade and increasing competitiveness of regional industries, but the public sector in Benin identified the ISRT Guarantee Bond and Logbook (also widely known by its French name: Carnet TRIE) documents as defunct. At the same time, two out of three private-sector respondents said they use the ISRT Logbook because it is necessary for cross-border trade, so they are using it in other countries. When traders must pay bonds at every border and then struggle to get the money returned, they become more likely to offer informal payments for passage, which ultimately reduces income to the government, producer, and driver and increases the costs of the goods to consumers
Benin	**NTBs:** Traders of a variety of goods are exposed to unoficial, unrecorded and arbitrary bans, quotas, and quantitative and seasonal restrictions, which are all in violation of ETLS protocols. Oficially, there is also an obligatory escort service for transit goods despite a well functioning container-seal system and a trucking syndicate that reduces competitive pricing for transport operations. Finally, road harassment is considerable in Benin, as private sector respondents indicate that a significant amount of fees are collected.

Benin	**Certificate of Origin:** Both public- and private-sector respondents noted the lack of confidence in Certificates of Origin from ECOWAS Member States. Applications for Certificates of Origin are not uniform across borders – different organizations issue different certificates of origin in different countries, they said. The issue of fake Certificates of Origin also complicates the entire process. Nigeria, for example, sometimes questions Certificates of Origin emanating from Benin, according torespondents, even from an ETLS-approved company. In such cases, Nigeria conducts separate investigations on the products before approving passage of trucks, immediately slowing passage, contradictin the processes and purposes of the ETLS-approved company scheme, and retarding regional integration.
Côte d'Ivoire	**Public sector oficials have insuficient or inconsistent information on the ETLS:** The public sector in Côte d'Ivoire was generally knowledgeable about ECOWAS protocols on the movement of persons, goods and transport, however, more emphasis was placed on UEMOA rules and procedures.
Côte d'Ivoire	**The private sector is sceptical of the ETLS and burdened by high and unpredictable trading costs:** Businesses in Côte d'Ivoire stated that many meetings are planned regarding the free movement of goods and vehicles, yet no progress has been made to that effect. The political will to resolve these issues is still lacking.

Côte d'Ivoire	**Incomplete implementation of the ETLS causes significant barriers to increased trade:** The Côte d'Ivoire study found significant gaps between oficial reported policy and traders' experience of bringing goods across the country's borders. Inconsistent application of policies and procedures makes trading costs unpredictable, and discourages investment and business expansion.
Ghana	**Application of Duty by Customs on ECOWAS Originating Goods:** The most important area of non-compliance with ETLS protocols involves the application of duties to ECOWAS originating goods as reported by the private sector. Ghana applies a host of other legal fees and taxes which add substantial costs to the conduct of trade. These additional taxes and fees are not part of the ETLS but they do affect the competitiveness of West African goods and the cost of goods to consumers.
Ghana	**Non-tariff Barriers including Seasonal and Quota Restrictions:** The second most significant area of non-implementation of ETLS protocols which merits attention relates to merchandise that is banned from importation or restricted by quotas.2 Only a few items are subject to these restrictions but they tend to be unprocessed agricultural items, which are exported from other Member States which could have a positive impact on their respective economies if allowed to be traded freely. Moreover, these items are often restricted for many months at a time and often treated inconsistently by customs oficials. Other areas where lack of implementation of the ETLS has an impact is in transportation and the movement of goods.
Côte d'Ivoire	

Ghana	**Three overarching challenges prevent the full operation of ETLS protocols in Ghana:** 1. The private sector is aware of the protocols but dissatisfied with the pace of implementation and has an attitude that informality may be less costly in time and money than strict adherence to the rules. 2. Complex and duplicative border procedures encourage incentives for informal trade. 3. Low earnings for public servants in trade and transport along with broader implementation of Ghana's newly established integrity program. The integrity program was designed to provide incentives to customs oficers for trade facilitation and respect within the public sector to act as a role model for wiping out corruption.
Mali	**Streamlining trading procedures and paperwork at each ECOWAS border:** Streamlining procedures and paperwork will lower import and export costs for domestic traders and consumers. As economists have shown, the bureaucratic costs can have similar effects to formal tariffs. Were the ETLS programs for cross-border trade of goods, transit and guarantees to function as envisaged, for example, they would improve Mali's access to regional markets by promoting freer and less-encumbered trade while mitigating insurance risks.

Mali	**Specialized training for government and private sector oficials on how to assess and clear merchandise that might qualify for preferential access under ECOWAS protocols:** Trainings should cover a summary of the benefits of a free trade agreement as well as a thorough explanation of how to implement different ETLS protocols. Efforts, such as the USAID West African Trade Hub's road transport corruption reports and this Gap Analysis, inform ECOWAS countries about the impediments to free trade within the region. Regular and thorough monitoring of the region's trade and transportation barriers will highlight progress as it is made
Mali	**Harmonization of UEMOA and ECOWAS Rules or Protocols:** It is unclear whether UEMOA or ECOWAS rules or protocols supersede one another. Currently, UEMOA rules are being followed. To encourage implementation of ECOWAS protocols, it is necessary to simplify ECOWAS protocols to help make them more applicable and relevant to the realities on the ground. A simple document summarizing selected ECOWAS/UEMOA protocols could also show samples of important documents. For dissemination at border points, a large billboard or a radio program summarizing requirements for illiterate truck drivers and travelers would be very useful.
Nigeria	**Quantity, quota and seasonal restrictions:** While public sector trade oficials deny there are any restrictions, the private sector reports they do exist, and have a significant impact on trade

Nigeria	**Non-tariff barriers:** These include non-reciprocity for standards/certifications; road harassment; and unoficial fees and delays, which were reported by private sector traders
Nigeria	**Duty charged on duty free goods:** Goods in transit are not supposed to be charged duty under ETLS protocols, which greatly increases costs.
Nigeria	**Improper use of transit documents and procedures:** The ISRT Logbook, vehicle inspections, customs bonds and permits are all used improperly in Nigeria, and add to time, cost and risk for traders
Nigeria	**There are three cross-cutting issues preventing the full operation of ETLS protocols in Nigeria, and which have a direct impact on all aspects of intra-regional trade:** 1. The gap between legislation and implementation—many ETLS protocols are codified in legislation, but there is a lack of enforcement and consistency in application at the borders. 2. Lack of awareness—private sector traders indicated they had limited, detailed information on ETLS protocols. 3. Incentives for informal trade— complex and duplicative border procedures that involve a significant level of harassment, which encourages informal methods of trade.

Senegal	**There are two cross-cutting issues preventing the full operation of ETLS protocols in Senegal and directly impacting all aspects of intra-regional trade:** 1. Gap between Legislation and Implementation: Many ETLS protocols are codified in legislation, but there is a lack of enforcement and consistency in application at the borders. In addition, unoficial non-tariff barriers are occasionally imposed at borders. 2. Low Private Sector Awareness of ETLS: Private sector traders indicated they had limited detailed information on ETLS protocols.
Senegal	**ISRT Guarantee Bond and Logbook are not functioning:** Private sector respondents requested that these protocols be re-instituted in Senegal. Currently, they need to pay for bank guarantee bonds, which are much more expensive than the ISRT Guarantee Bond.
Senegal	**Non-Tariff Barriers:** Traders of a variety of agricultural goods are exposed to unoficial, unrecorded, seemingly arbitrary bans, quotas, and quantitative and seasonal restrictions, which are all in violation of ETLS protocols. In addition, there is an obligatory escort service for transit goods despite a well-functioning container seal system. Finally, road harassment is a noteworthy concern in Senegal, as private sector respondents indicated that significant amounts of fees are collected.

| Togo | **There are two cross-cutting issues preventing the full operation of ETLS protocols in Togo, and which have a direct impact on all aspects of intra-regional trade:**
1. Gap between Legislation and Implementation: The Team was unable to find updated legislation, regulation or procedures that addressed many of the ETLS protocol. As in many countries there is a lack of enforcement and consistency in application at the borders. In addition, there are instances where unoficial non-tariff barriers are imposed at the borders.

2. Low Private Sector Awareness of ETLS: Private sector traders indicated they had limited, detailed information on ETLS protocols, their rights where to find information related to documents that should be needed for transit across borders and the normal fees for processing. |
| Togo | **ISRT Guarantee Bond and Log Book are not functioning:**
Although two out of three Private sector respondents said they use the log book and it is necessary for cross border trade, it is probably for trade in other countries since the public sector in Togo identified these documents as defunct. ECOWAS must have a uniform customs transit, declaration and bond system such as the ISRT to function properly and increase the competitiveness of their industries. |

Togo	**Non-tariff barriers:** Traders of a variety of goods are exposed to arbitrary bans, quotas, quantitative and seasonal restrictions, which are all in violation of ETLS protocols, but are unoficial, and not recorded. In addition, there is an obligatory escort service for transit goods despite a well-functioning container seal system and the trucking syndicate reduces competitive pricing for transport operations. Finally, road harassment is a noteworthy concern in Togo, as private sector respondents indicate that a significant amount of fees are collected.